CHRISTOPHER D. STONE, Professor of Law at the University of Southern California, attended Harvard University and graduated *magna cum laude* in Philosophy. After receiving his law degree from Yale, he was Fellow in Law and Economics at the University of Chicago. He then practiced law with a large Wall Street firm until he moved to California to join the faculty at U.S.C., teaching courses that range from Legal Philosophy to Corporate Law. A past Chairman of the Association of American Law School's Committee on Law and the Humanities, Professor Stone is also a member of the American Society for Political and Legal Philosophy and has served as Consultant to the President's Task Force on Communications Policy. He is the author of LAW, LANGUAGE, AND ETHICS; and is currently working on a major study of the problems involved in the social control of the modern business corporation.

Special Revised Edition

SHOULD TREES HAVE STANDING?

TOWARD LEGAL RIGHTS FOR NATURAL OBJECTS

CHRISTOPHER D. STONE

 DISCUS BOOKS/PUBLISHED BY AVON

AVON BOOKS
A division of
The Hearst Corporation
959 Eighth Avenue
New York, New York 10019

Library of Congress Catalog Card Number: 75–29592

ISBN: 0-380-00400-3

First Discus Printing, October, 1975

Printed in the U.S.A.

For my little hiking companions:
Jessica and Carey

Contents

❧ FOREWORD

From our ancestors we inherit three sorts of things: material objects, genes, and ideas. Of those three the first is least important, for "a fool and his money are soon parted." The other two inheritances leave more lasting traces. Genes and ideas are both stable as a rule, but the rule is normally broken at a low frequency. Genes and ideas are both mutable. The diversity created by change constitutes the field in which the forces of selection operate. On the biological plane selection is called "natural," and the result is judged "adaptation." Selection at the level of ideas goes by various names, "criticism" and "rational evaluation" among them; the results are generally referred to as "progress" (which they may indeed sometimes be).

The mutation of ideas differs strikingly from the mutation of genes in this way: change in an idea by which we have previously been unconsciously ruled becomes much more probable once the idea has been explicitly brought out into the open. Such a change in changeability does not hold for genes. The gene for the normal alternative to the disease hemophilia mutates to hemophilic form about once in every fifty thousand opportunities, with Olympian indifference to our awareness of it.

In the mental realm, to express an idea clearly is to invite its denial. Our lives are no doubt ruled tyrannically by a wealth of ideas we have no idea of—until, without warning, we become aware of them one by one. As each ruling idea surfaces it becomes subject to a mutation process that is faster by many orders of magnitude than is the natural mutation of genes.

The foregoing assertions may sound suspiciously like the elements of a "waterproof hypothesis," since they assert the existence of unconscious forces that lose their force once they cease to be unconscious. Such a postulation would seem to be beyond proof or disproof; if so, we should refuse it admission to the realm of rational discourse. But I think the postulation is better than that. *Looking backward* we can see that we—and by "we" I mean both ourselves and the ancestors with whom we psychologically affiliate ourselves—were formerly ruled by ideas that "we" were unconscious of at the time when the rule was effective. For example, the "divine right of kings" was calmly accepted before the phrase was invented. The invention of a legitimating phrase is often the first step to doubt and the opening of a door to the exploration of alternatives. He who explicitly asserts that kings

2

have a divine right to rule cannot keep others from asking, "But how do you know that? And what if they don't? What would the world be like then?" In fact, the speaker cannot shield even himself against subterranean doubts once he has been so imprudent as to make a ruling assumption explicit.

Aware of tyrannical ideas we escaped in the past we cannot but wonder what unconscious ideas rule us still. How can we discover them, and so take one more step in the endless journey of escape from intellectual tyranny? There is no royal road to the discovery of the unconscious, but the economist John Maynard Keynes blazed a useful trail when he said that "a study of the history of opinion is a necessary preliminary to the emancipation of the mind." Becoming aware of the indefensible in the mental baggage of our ancestors we become sensitized to that which is dubious in our own minds.

The American naturalist Aldo Leopold opened the way to escape from one of the ideological tyrannies of our time when he made us acutely aware of the hidden implications of the terms "rights" and "property," by recounting the history recorded in the myths of Homer:

> When god-like Odysseus returned from the wars in Troy, he hanged all on one rope a dozen slave-girls of his household whom he suspected of misbehavior during his absence.

This hanging involved no question of propriety. The girls were property. The disposal of property was then, as now, a matter of expediency, not of right and wrong.

Concepts of right and wrong were not lacking from Odysseus' Greece: witness the fidelity of his wife through the long years before at last his black-prowed galleys clove the wine-dark seas for home. The ethical structure of that day covered wives, but had not yet been extended to human chattels. During the three thousand years which have since elapsed, ethical criteria have been extended to many fields of conduct, with corresponding shrinkages in those judged by expediency only.

This extension of ethics, so far studied only by philosophers, is actually a process in ecological evolution. Its sequences may be described in ecological as well as in philosophical terms. An ethic, ecologically, is a limitation on freedom of action in the struggle for existence. An ethic, philosophically, is a differentiation of social from anti-social conduct. These are two definitions of one thing. The thing has its origin in the tendency of interdependent individuals or groups to evolve modes of co-operation. The ecologist calls these symbioses. Politics and economics are advanced symbioses in which the original free-for-all competition has been replaced, in part, by co-operative mechanisms with an ethical content.

This passage,* from the essay "The Land Ethic," first published posthumously in 1949, has been often reprinted. The essay has had a great effect, first on biologists and ecologists, and latterly on the general public. Leopold went on to say:

> There is as yet no ethic dealing with man's relation to land and to the animals and plants which grow upon it. Land, like Odysseus' slave-girls, is still property. The land-relation is still strictly economic, entailing privileges but not obligations.
>
> The extension of ethics to this third element in the human environment is, if I read the evidence correctly, an evolutionary possibility and an ecological necessity. . . . Individual thinkers since the days of Ezekiel and Isaiah have asserted that the despoliation of land is not only inexpedient but wrong. Society, however, has not yet affirmed their belief. I regard the present conservation movement as the embryo of such an affirmation.
>
> An ethic may be regarded as a mode of

* Taken from page 217 of Aldo Leopold, *A Sand County Almanac*. New York: Oxford University Press, 1966.

guidance for meeting ecological situations so new or intricate, or involving such deferred reactions, that the path of social expediency is not discernible to the average individual. Animal instincts are modes of guidance for the individual in meeting such situations. Ethics are possibly a kind of community instinct in-the-making.

The animal instincts Leopold refers to include the territorial behavior of higher animals. Animal territoriality is no doubt the progenitor of the human concept of "property," a concept which has, like all things human, undergone a wealth of variations. Asserting that property is natural in its origin does not justify any and all of these variations. Equally natural is the concern for the welfare of other human beings that periodically brings the rights of property into question.

The most rigid defenders of the momentary legal definition of "property" apparently think "property" refers to something as substantive as atom and mass. But every good lawyer and every good economist knows that "property" is not a *thing* but merely a verbal announcement that certain traditional powers and privileges of some members of society will be vigorously defended against attack by others. Operationally, the word "property" symbolizes a threat of action; it is a verb-like entity, but (being a noun) the word biases our thoughts toward the substantives we call *things*. But the permanence enjoyed by property is not the permanence of an atom, but that of a promise (a most unsubstantial thing). Even after we become aware of the misdirection of attention enforced by the noun "property," we may still passively acquiesce to the inaccuracy of its continued use because a degree of social stability is needed to get the day-to-day work accomplished. But when it becomes painfully clear that the continued unthinking use of the word "property" is leading to consequences that are obviously unjust and socially counterproductive, then we must stop short and ask ourselves how we want to redefine the rights of property.

Law, to be stable, must be based on ethics. In evoking a new ethic to protect land and other natural amenities, Leopold implicitly called for concomitant changes in the philosophy of the law. Now, less than a generation after the publication of Leopold's classic essay, Professor Christopher D. Stone has laid the foundation for just such a philosophy in a graceful essay that itself bids fair to become a classic. The occasion of its writing was the preparation of a special issue of the *Southern California Law Review* devoted to "Law and Technology," which was published as Volume 45, Number 2 in the spring of 1972. Professor Stone later explained the background to me in detail:

"For some time I have been thinking about the interplay between law and the development of social awareness, emphasizing to my students that societies, like human beings, progress through different stages of sensitiveness, and that in our progress through these stages the law—like art—has a role to play, dramatizing and summoning into the open the changes that are taking place within us. While exemplifying this in class and trying to imagine what a future consciousness might look like, I began to discuss the idea of nature or natural objects being regarded as the subjects of legal rights.

"The students were—to say the least—skeptical. After all, it is easy to say, 'Nature should have legal rights,' but if the notion were ever to be more than a vague sentiment, I had to find some pending case in which nature's having legal rights would make a real operational difference.

"It was in this context that I turned to the Mineral King case, then recently decided by the Ninth Circuit Court of Appeals. The U.S. Forest Service had granted a permit to Walt Disney Enterprises, Inc. to 'develop' Mineral King Valley, a wilderness area in California's Sierra Nevada Mountains, by construction of a $35 million complex of motels, restaurants, and recreational facilities. The Sierra Club, maintaining that the project would adversely affect the area's esthetic and ecological balance, brought suit for an injunction. The District Court had granted a preliminary injunction. But the Ninth Circuit reversed. The key to the Ninth Circuit's opinion was this: not that the Forest Service had been right in granting the permit, but that the Sierra Club had no "standing" to bring the question to the courts. After all, the Ninth Circuit reasoned, the Sierra Club itself

does not allege that it is "aggrieved" or that it is "adversely affected" within the meaning of the rules of standing. Nor does the fact that no one else appears on the scene who is in fact aggrieved and is willing or desirous of taking up the cudgels create a right in appellee. The right to sue does not inure to one who does not possess it, simply because there is no one willing and able to assert it.

"This, I saw at once, was the needed case, a ready-made vehicle to bring to the Court's attention the theory I was developing. Perhaps the injury to the Sierra Club was tenuous, but the injury to Mineral King—the park itself—wasn't. If I could get the courts thinking about the park itself as a jural person— the way corporations are "persons"—the notion of nature having rights would here make a significant operational difference—the difference between the case being heard and (the way things were then heading) thrown out of court.

"It was October 1971. The Sierra Club's appeal had already been docketed for review by the United States Supreme Court. The case, we calculated, would be up for argument in November or December at the latest. Was it possible that we could get an article out in time to influence, perhaps, the course of the law? I sat down with Dave Boutte, then the editor of the *Southern California Law Review*, and we made some quick estimates. The next issue of the *Review* to go to press would be a special Symposium on Law and Technology, which was scheduled for publication in late March or early April. There was no hope, then, of getting an article out in time for the lawyers to work the idea into their briefs or oral arguments. Could it be published in time for the Justices to see it before they had finished deliberating and writing their opinions? The chances that the case would still be undecided in April were only slim. But there was one hope. Justice Douglas (who, if anyone on the Court, might be receptive to the notion of legal rights for natural objects) was scheduled to write the Preface to the Symposium on Law and Technology. For this reason he would be supplied with a draft of all the manuscripts in December. Thus he would at least have this idea in his hands. If the case were long enough in the deciding, and if he found the theory convincing, he might even have the article available as a source of support.

"We decided to try it. Dave made some last-minute room for my article in the Symposium and I pulled it together at a pace that, as such academic writings go, was almost break-neck. The manuscripts for the Symposium issue went to the printer in late December, and then began a long wait; the two of us hoping that—at least in this case— the wheels of justice would turn slowly. Our excitement at what happened next I leave to you to imagine."

What happened next was that the Mineral King decision was held up until 19 April 1972. On that date the United States Supreme Court (the new appointees Powell and Rehnquist not participating) upheld the Ninth Circuit. The Sierra Club itself had no sufficient "personal stake in the outcome of the controversy" to get into Court. Stone's theory (or some alternate) not having been raised, Justice Stewart, writing for the majority, did not feel called upon to pass upon its validity. But in a footnote, he dropped a broad hint: "Our decision does not, of course, bar the Sierra Club from seeking in the District

Court to amend its complaint by a motion" invoking some other theory of jurisdiction.

Then came Justice Douglas's dissent. Although the theory of nature itself being the rights-holder had not been pleaded, he decided to deal with it then and there. In his very opening paragraph—which was to resound in newspapers and editorials across the country—he proclaimed:

> The critical question of "standing" would be simplified and also put neatly in focus if we fashioned a federal rule that allowed environmental issues to be litigated before federal agencies or federal courts in the name of the inanimate object about to be despoiled, defaced, or invaded by roads and bulldozers and where injury is the subject of public outrage. Contemporary public concern for protecting nature's ecological equilibrium should lead to the conferral of standing upon environmental objects to sue for their own preservation. See Stone, Should Trees Have Standing? Toward Legal Rights for Natural Objects, 45 S. Cal. L. Rev. 450 (1972). This suit would therefore be more properly labeled as *Mineral King v. Morton.*

Douglas was not alone. Theretofore Justice Blackmun (a Nixon appointee) had been in agreement with Justice Douglas on a major issue perhaps only once, but the two were brought together on this. Blackmun endorsed the idea in the following terms:

> . . . Mr. Justice Douglas, in his eloquent opinion, has imaginatively suggested another means [to establish standing] and one, in its own way, with obvious, appropriate and self-imposed limitations. . . . As I read what he has written, he makes only one addition to the customary criteria (the existence of a genuine dispute; the assurance of adversariness; and a conviction that the party whose standing is challenged will adequately represent the interests he asserts), that is, that the litigant be one who speaks knowingly for the environmental values he asserts.

Justice Brennan agreed.

Thus, when the dust settled, three justices had endorsed the notion and would have "interpreted" the Sierra Club's complaint as though it had been intended to raise Stone's thesis (conceiving Mineral King as the party in interest and the Sierra Club as its guardian). Two judges not on the Court at the time of the argument had abstained, and the other four (a bare majority) had chosen not to reach the theory because it had not, technically speaking, been raised.

In a way, the trees lost, albeit narrowly—and

perhaps temporarily. Had they won, the Mineral King decision would no doubt have been called a "watershed decision." A watershed—the topographical image must be kept in mind—is ordinarily recognized only after one has passed over the ridge and is ambling down the other side. (If we haven't passed the ridge, how do we know there is one?) In the present instance, however, I submit that it is a good bet that we are near the ridge of a watershed. It is not merely the closeness of the decision (4-to-3) that leads to the suspicion; it is also the tone of the majority opinion—which is not unfriendly to the trees—as well as other evidences of a changing climate of opinion in this country. Within a month of the court's decision Senator Philip A. Hart of Michigan praised Stone's article on the floor of the Senate and received permission to have it reprinted in the Congressional Record. The rapidity with which Stone's work has been favorably commented on by jurists, journalists, and legislators gives grounds for optimism as to the early incorporation into law of Stone's thesis that natural objects should have standing in court.

Justice Blackmun, at the conclusion of his opinion, calls attention to the deep reason why change is called for when he quotes the famous lines from John Donne, "No man is an Iland. . . ." (See p. 94) The poet's rhetoric does not automatically give us answers to the thousand and one practical questions with which we are daily confronted, but it does furnish a framework within which acceptable solutions may be found, namely the ecological framework. The world is a seamless web of interrelationships within which no part can, without danger, claim absolute sovereignty in rights over all other parts. Even those who agree (as not all do) with Alexander Pope that "Man is the measure of all things" must admit that man's interests are sometimes served best by taking seriously Christ's advice: "Consider the lilies of the field. . . . They toil not, neither do they spin: and yet I say unto you that even Solomon in all his glory was not arrayed like one of these." Even the narrowest view of the interests of mankind, if pursued to its farthest bound, leads us to conclude that our greatest happiness, especially if we are mindful of the survival in dignity of our posterity, demands that we give some sort of standing in court to the lilies, the trees, and all the other glories of nature.

"Poets," said Shelley, "are the unacknowledged legislators of the world." During the last two centuries the words of William Blake, William Wordsworth, Henry David Thoreau, John Muir, John Burroughs, Rachel Carson, Aldo Leopold, and a host of others have been giving form to the statute books of our unconscious minds. But that which is unconscious is seldom precise, and in any case is not suited for action in a world of differing opinions. The statute law of the moment that is precise enough

15

for action does not adequately take into account what many of us see as our responsibilities as trustees of the earth. Surely it is time now to make explicit the implications of the poets' insights and rebuild the written law "nearer to the heart's desire."

GARRETT HARDIN

Santa Barbara
December 1973

INTRODUCTION:
The Unthinkable

In *The Descent of Man,* written a full century ago, Charles Darwin observed that the history of man's moral development has been a continual extension in the range of objects receiving his "social instincts and sympathies." Originally each man had moral concern only for himself and those of a very narrow circle about him; later, he came to regard more and more "not only the welfare, but the happiness of all his fellow men." Then, gradually, "his sympathies became more tender and widely diffused, extending to men of all races, to the imbecile, maimed and other useless members of society, and finally to the lower animals. . . ."

The history of the law suggests a parallel development. The scope of "things" accorded legal protection has been continuously extending. Members of the earliest "families" (including extended kinship groups and clans) treated everyone on the outside as suspect, alien, and rightless, except in the vacant sense of each man's "right to self-defense." "An Indian Thug," it has been written, "conscientiously regretted that he had not robbed and strangled as many travelers as did his father before him. In a rude state of civilization the robbery of strangers is, indeed, generally considered as honorable." And even within a single family, persons we presently regard as the natural holders of at least some legal rights had none. Take, for example, children. We know something of the early rights-status of children from the widespread practice of infanticide—especially of the deformed and female. (Senicide, practiced by the North American Indians, was the corresponding rightlessness of the aged.) Sir Henry Maine tells us that as late as the *Patria Potestas* of the Romans, the father had *jus vitae necisque*—the power of life and death—over his children. It followed legally, Maine writes, that

> [he had power] of uncontrolled corporal chastisement; he can modify their personal condition at pleasure; he can give a wife to his son; he can give his daughter in marriage; he can divorce his children of either sex; he can transfer them to another family by adoption; and he can sell them.

The child was less than a person: it was, in the eyes of the law, an object, a thing.

The legal rights of children have long since

been recognized in principle, and are still expanding in practice. Witness, just within recent time, *In re Gault*, the United States Supreme Court decision guaranteeing basic constitutional protections to juvenile defendants, and the Voting Rights Act of 1970, with its lowering of the voting age to eighteen. We have been making persons of children although they were not, in law, always so. And we have done the same, albeit imperfectly some would say, with prisoners, aliens, women (married women, especially, were nonpersons through most of legal history), the insane, blacks, fetuses, and Indians.

People are apt to suppose that there are natural limits on how far the law can go, that it is only matter in human form that can come to be recognized as the possessor of rights. But it simply is not so. The world of the lawyer is peopled with inanimate right-holders: trusts, corporations, joint ventures, municipalities, Subchapter R partnerships, and nation-states, to mention just a few. Ships, still referred to by courts in the feminine gender, have long had an independent jural life, often with striking consequences. In one famous U.S. Supreme Court case a ship had been seized and used by pirates. After the ship's capture, the owners asked for her return; after all, the vessel had been pressed into piracy without their knowledge or consent. But the United States condemned and sold the "offending vessel." In denying release to the owners,

Justice Story quoted Chief Justice Marshall from an earlier case:

> This is not a proceeding against the owner; it is a proceeding against the vessel for an offense committed by the vessel; which is not the less an offense ... because it was committed without the authority and against the will of the owner.

The *ship* was, in the eyes of the law, the guilty person.

We have become so accustomed to the idea of a corporation having "its" own rights, and being a "person" and "citizen" for so many statutory and constitutional purposes, that we forget how perplexing the notion was to early jurists. "That invisible, intangible and artificial being, that mere legal entity," Chief Justice Marshall wrote of the corporation in *Bank of the United States v. Deveaux*—could a suit be brought in its name? Ten years later, in the *Dartmouth College* case, he was still refusing to let pass unnoticed the wonder of an entity "existing only in contemplation of law." Yet, long before Marshall worried over the personification of the modern corporation, the best medieval legal scholars had spent hundreds of years struggling with the legal nature of those great public "corporate bodies," the Church and the State. How could they exist in law, as entities transcending the living pope and king? It was clear how a king could bind himself—on his honor—by a treaty. But when the king died, what was it that was burdened with the obligations of, and claimed the rights under, the treaty his tangible hand had signed? The medieval mind saw (what we have lost our capacity to see) how unthinkable it was, and worked out the most elaborate conceits and fallacies to serve as anthropomorphic flesh for the Universal Church and the Universal Empire.

It is this note of the unthinkable that I want to dwell upon for a moment. Throughout legal history, each successive extension of rights to some new entity has been, theretofore, a bit unthinkable. Every era is inclined to suppose the rightlessness of its rightless "things" to be a decree of Nature, not a legal convention—an open social choice—acting in support of some status quo. It is thus that we avoid coming face to face with all the moral, social, and economic dimensions of what *we* are doing. Consider, for example, how the United States Supreme Court sidestepped the moral issues behind slavery in its 1856 *Dred Scott* decision: blacks had been denied the rights of citizenship "as a subordinate and inferior class of beings." Their unfortunate legal status reflected, in other words, not our choice at all, but "just the way things were." In an 1856 contest over a will, the deceased's provision that his slaves should decide between emancipation and public sale was held void on the ground that slaves had no legal capacity to choose. "These decisions," the Virginia court explained,

> are legal conclusions flowing naturally and necessarily from the one clear, simple, fundamental idea of chattel slavery. That fundamental idea is, that, in the eye of the law, so far certainly as civil rights and relations are concerned, the slave is not a person, but a thing. The investiture of a chattel with civil rights or legal capacity is indeed a legal solecism and absurdity. The attribution of a legal personality to a chattel slave,— legal conscience, legal intellect, legal freedom, or liberty and power of free choice and action, and corresponding legal obligations growing out of such qualities, faculties and action—implies a palpable contradiction in terms.

In a like vein, the highest court in California once explained that Chinese had not the right to testify against white men in criminal matters because they were "a race of people whom nature has marked as inferior, and who are incapable of progress or intellectual development beyond a certain point ... between whom and ourselves nature has placed an impassable difference."

The popular conception of the Jew in the thirteenth century contributed to a law which treated them, as one legal commentator has observed, as "men *ferae naturae*, protected by a quasi-forest law. Like the roe and the deer, they form an order apart." Recall, too, that it was not so long ago that the fetus was "like the roe and the deer." In an early suit attempting to establish a wrongful death action on behalf of a negligently killed fetus (now widely accepted practice in American courts), Holmes, then on the Massachusetts Supreme Court, seems to have thought it simply inconceivable "that a man might owe a civil duty and incur a conditional prospective liability in tort to one not yet in being." The first woman in Wisconsin who thought she might have a right to practice law was told that she did not. *We* had nothing against *them*, of course; but they were *naturally* different.

> The law of nature destines and qualifies the female sex for the bearing and nurture of the children of our race and for the custody of the homes of the world ... [A]ll lifelong callings of women, inconsistent with these radical and sacred duties of their sex, as is the profession of the law, are departures from the order of nature; and when voluntary, treason against it. . . . The peculiar qualities of womanhood, its gentle graces, its quick sensibility, its tender susceptibility, its purity, its delicacy, its emotional impulses, its subordination of hard reason to sympathetic feeling, are surely not qualifications for forensic strife. Nature has

23

tempered woman as little for the juridical conflicts of the court room, as for the physical conflicts of the battle field. . . .

The fact is, that each time there is a movement to confer rights onto some new "entity," the proposal is bound to sound odd or frightening or laughable.* This is partly because until the rightless thing receives its rights, we cannot see it as anything but a thing for the use of "us"—those who are holding rights at the time.

---

* Recently, a group of prison inmates in Suffolk County tamed a mouse that they discovered, giving him the name Morris. Discovering Morris, a jailer flushed him down the toilet. The prisoners brought a proceeding against the warden complaining, *inter alia*, that Morris was subjected to discriminatory discharge and was otherwise unequally treated. The action was unsuccessful, the court noting that the inmates themselves were "guilty of imprisoning Morris without a charge, without a trial, and without bail," and that other mice at the prison were not treated more favorably. "As to the true victim, the Court can only offer again the sympathy first proffered to his ancestors by Robert Burns's poem, "To a Mouse."

The whole matter seems humorous, of course. But we need to know more of the function of humor in the unfolding of a culture, and the ways in which it is involved with the social growing pains to which it is testimony. Why do people make jokes about the Women's Liberation Movement? Is it not on account of—rather than in spite of—the underlying validity of the protests and the uneasy awareness that a recognition of the claims is inevitable? Arthur Koestler rightly begins his study of the human mind, *Act of Creation* (1964), with an analysis of humor, entitled "The Logic of Laughter." Cf. Freud's paper, "Jokes and the Unconscious."

(Thus it was that the Founding Fathers could speak of the inalienable rights of all men, and yet maintain a society that was, by modern standards, without the most basic rights for blacks, Indians, children and women. There was no hypocrisy; emotionally, no one felt that these other things were *men*.) In this vein, what is striking about the Wisconsin case above is that the court, for all its talk about women, so clearly was never able to see women as they are and might become. All it could see was the popular "idealized" version of an object it needed. Such is the way the slave South looked upon the black. "The older South," W. E. DuBois wrote, clung to "the sincere and passionate belief that somewhere between men and cattle, God created a *tertium quid,* and called it a Negro."

Obviously, there is something of a seamless web involved: there will be resistance to giving a "thing" rights until it can be seen and valued for itself; yet, it is hard to see it and value a "thing" for itself until we can bring ourselves to give it rights—which is almost inevitably going to sound inconceivable to a large group of people.

The reader must know by now, if only from the title of the book, the reason for this little discourse on the unthinkable. I am quite seriously proposing that we recognize legal rights of forests, oceans, rivers and other so-called "natural objects" in the environment—indeed, of the natural environment as a whole.

As strange as such a notion may sound, it is neither fanciful nor without considerable operational significance. In fact, I do not think it would be a misdescription of recent developments in the law to say that we are already on the verge of such an assignment of rights to nature, although we have not faced up to what we are doing in those particular terms.

We should do so now, and begin to explore the implications such an idea would yield.

CHRISTOPHER D. STONE

ONE

What It Means To
Have Legal Rights

To say that the natural environment should
have rights is not to say anything as silly as that
no one should be allowed to cut down a tree.
We say human beings have rights, but—at least
as of the time of this writing—they may be executed. Corporations have rights, but they cannot plead the Fifth Amendment; the case of *In
re Gault* gave fifteen-year-olds certain rights in
juvenile proceedings, but it did not give them
the right to vote. In the same way, to say that
the environment should have rights is not to say
that it should have every right we can imagine,
or even the same body of rights as human
beings have. Nor is it to say that every thing in
the environment should have the same rights as
every other thing in the environment.

Fundamentally, the granting of legal rights to
the environment would have consequences in

two areas. First, there would be certain changes in the operation of the legal system—in the ways in which environmental claims would be treated judicially. Second, there would be significant ramifications throughout the society—subtler changes that I expect would touch individual personality structures and the overall social consciousness. I shall deal with these two aspects in turn.

THE OPERATIONAL SIGNIFICANCE OF HOLDING LEGAL RIGHTS

There is, to begin with, a lack of understanding of what it means to have "legal rights." Let me indicate how I shall be using the expression here.

First and most obviously, if the term is to have any content at all, no one can be said to have a *right* unless there is some glimmer of hope for a *remedy*: for some public authoritative body (a court, an administrative agency) to give some amount of review to actions that seem to encroach upon that "right." For example, a student may say—speaking loosely—that he has a "right" to his education. But speaking more strictly, if he can be expelled from his university and cannot get any public official, even a judge or administrative agent at the lowest level, either (i) to require the university to justify its actions (if only to the extent of filling out an affidavit alleging that the expulsion "was not wholly arbitrary and capricious") or (ii) to compel the university to accord the student some procedural safeguards (a hearing, right to counsel, right to have notice of charges), then in a real, operational sense, it is simply misdescriptive to say he has a legal right to his education (rather than, perhaps, a moral claim).

Thus, for a thing to be a holder of legal rights, nothing is more basic than that there be in the social structure some authoritative body prepared to review and call to question the actions of those who threaten it. But that isn't all. As I shall use the term, "holder of legal rights," each of three additional criteria must be satisfied. All three, one will observe, go towards making a thing count jurally—to have a legally recognized worth and dignity in its own right, and not merely to serve as a means to benefit "us" (whoever the contemporary group of rights-holders may be). They are

• first, that the thing can institute legal actions at *its* behest—to have what the lawyer calls *standing;*

• second, that in determining whether to grant legal relief, the court must take *its* injuries into account; and

• third, that relief must run to *its* benefit.

To illustrate, consider two hypothetical societies each of which condons slavery; let's simply call the societies S_1 and S_2. Suppose now that under the laws of S_1, if someone beats a slave, the slave's master can (if *he* chooses) go to court, and the court will make the defendant pay *him* the reduced value *to him* of his slave's lost labors. (If, for example, the slave has lost the use of an arm, the damages will be measured by the reduction in his productive worth to the master.) Contrast this with the laws of S_2, in which *the slave* can institute the proceedings himself (whether his master approves of the lawsuit or not) for *his* own recovery, the measure of damages including, say, *his* pain and suffering. Notice that neither society is so structured as to leave wholly unprotected the slave's interests in not being beaten. But in S_2 as opposed to S_1, there are three operationally significant advantages that the slave has, and these make the slave in S_2, albeit a slave, a holder of rights.

Or, again, compare two societies, S_1, in which prenatal injury to a child who is subsequently liveborn gives a right of action against the wrongdoer at the mother's instance, for the mother's benefit, on the basis of the mother's mental anguish, and S_2, which gives the child a suit in *its* own name (through a legally appointed guardian) for *its* own recovery, for the damages *it* will suffer through life.

When I say, then, that at common law "natural objects" are not holders of legal rights, I am not simply remarking what we would all accept, without any reflection, as obvious. I mean to emphasize three specific legal-operational advantages that the environment lacks, leaving it in the position of the slave and the fetus in S_1, rather than the slave and fetus of S_2.

THE RIGHTLESSNESS OF NATURAL
OBJECTS AT COMMON LAW

Consider, for example, the common law's posture toward the pollution of a stream. True, courts have always been empowered, in extreme circumstances, to issue orders that will stop the pollution—just as the legal system in S_1 is so structured as incidentally to discourage beating slaves and being reckless around pregnant women. But the stream itself is fundamentally rightless, with implications that deserve careful reconsideration.

The first sense in which the stream is not a rights-holder has to do with *standing*—the power to institute legal actions when its interests dictate. The stream itself is legally voiceless. So far as the common law is concerned, the polluter's actions are not going to be challenged unless and until a lower riparian (the law's term for the owner of the land abutting the stream) is

31

willing and able to show an invasion of his own human rights—to demonstrate that *he* is suffering.

This conception of our legal system—that it is the riparian who holds the right to bring suit—has more than theoretical interest. It means that the pollution may go unchallenged. The lower riparians may simply not care about the pollution upstream. They themselves may be polluting, and not wish to stir up legal waters. They may be economically dependent on their polluting neighbor. (In at least one case, the California Supreme Court turned down the state attorney general's request to enjoin a polluter on the grounds that the lower riparian owners, most of whom were dependent on the lumbering business of the polluting mill, refused to complain.) And, of course, when the lower riparians discount the value of winning by what it costs to bring a lawsuit and the chances of success, the action may not seem worth undertaking. It may be, for example, that while a polluter is causing $100,000 a year damage to all the downstream owners in the aggregate, there are 1,000 owners involved, no one of which is suffering more than $100: who wants to press suit for $100? In those circumstances, and considering the increasing barriers to class actions, no one may even feel it worth the trouble and cost of securing co-plaintiffs.

The hesitancy of the human riparians to sue will be especially likely when they take into account, as an additional factor, the burdens the law puts in their way. In various jurisdictions it may be up to the plaintiff to prove that, given the present state of technology (of which he may know little) a practical means of pollution abatement exists; he may have to demonstrate the "specific damages" he suffered; to prove the "unreasonableness" of defendant's use of the water; to overcome difficulties raised by issues such as joint causality, the right to pollute by prescription*, and so forth. Even in states which, like California, have sought to give the environment a boost by empowering the attorney general to sue for pollution abatement, the power has been sparingly invoked and, when invoked, narrowly construed by the courts.

The second sense in which the common law denies "rights" to natural objects has to do with the way in which the merits of the case are decided. The question here is, even in those controversies in which someone is competent and willing to establish standing, how significantly are the injuries to the environment going to weigh in the final judgment? At its earliest stages, the legal system protected the "rights" of the property-owning human with minimal consideration of any other values, human or otherwise: *"Cujus est solum, ejus est usque ad*

---

* In other words, because the polluter had been doing it for so long, he has acquired a right to continue, the way in which a pathway can be created by easement over a neighbor's land.

coelum et ad infernos." ("Whoever owns the soil owns everything above it and below it.") "He [the landowner] may waste or despoil the land as he pleases . . ." Today the law is not so willing to let a man do whatever he pleases on his property, irrespective of the effects. But—and here is the crux of the matter—the balances courts strike are fundamentally aimed to adjust the competing human interests, rather than the interests among humans and the environment.

To continue with stream pollution as an example, there are commentators who speak of a "general rule" that "a riparian owner is legally entitled to have the stream flow by his land with its quality unimpaired"; they write that "an upper owner has, prima facie, no right to pollute the water." Such a doctrine, if strictly invoked, would protect the stream absolutely (even if derivatively) whenever a suit was brought on a human's behalf. But obviously, to look around us, that is not the result that the law is achieving. Almost everywhere there are doctrinal qualifications on the riparian's supposed "rights" to an unpolluted stream (someone's right, for example, to pollute "by prescription," i.e., because he's been doing it for a long time). Although these rules vary from jurisdiction to jurisdiction, and upon whether one is suing for an equitable injunction or for damages, what they all have in common is some sort of balancing. And whether the courts use the language of "reasonable use," "reasonable methods of use," "balance of convenience," or "the public interest doctrine," what the law is balancing, with varying degrees of directness, are the economic hardships on the upper riparian (or dependent community) of abating the pollution vis-à-vis the economic hardships on the lower riparians of continuing to put up with the pollution. Thus we find the highest court of Pennsylvania refusing to stop a coal company from discharging polluted mine water into a tributary of the Lackawana River because the plaintiff's "grievance is for a mere personal inconvenience; and ... mere private personal inconveniences ... must yield to the necessities of a great public industry, which although in the hands of a private corporation, subserves a great public interest." Such cases, in Judge Learned Hand's words, involve "a quantitative compromise between *two* conflicting interests." He meant, of course, the interests of one group of humans weighed off against the interests of another group of humans. What does not weigh in the balance is the damage to the stream itself, to its fish and turtles and "lower" life. So long as the natural environment itself is rightless, these are not matters for judicial cognizance.

The third way in which the common law makes natural objects rightless has to do with whom it regards as the beneficiary of a favorable judgment. Here, too, it makes a considerable difference that it is not the *natural object* that counts in its own right. To illustrate this

35

point, let me begin by observing that it makes perfectly good sense to speak of and ascertain the legal damage to a natural object, if only in the sense of "making it whole" with respect to the most obvious damages it is suffering. The costs of making a forest whole, for example, would include the costs of reseeding, repairing watersheds, restocking wildlife—the sorts of costs the Forest Service undertakes after a fire. Making a polluted stream whole would include the costs of restocking with fish, waterfowl, and other animal and vegetable life, dredging, washing out impurities, establishing natural and/or artificial aerating agents, and so forth.

What is important to note is that, under our present system, even if someone wins a water pollution suit for damages, all the polluter has to pay is what the pollution cost the plaintiff (the reduced resale value, say, of his land). No money has to be paid to the benefit of the stream itself, to repair *its* damages. This omission has the corollary effect that the potential damages the law confronts a polluter with—our threat to make him stop—may not be so much as to force him to desist, even where the *total injury* he is causing (the injury to the stream included) outweighs what the polluter's production is contributing to the society. For example, it is easy to imagine a polluter whose activities cause damages to the extent of $10,000 annually—$7,000 to the stream itself and $3,000 aggregate damage to all the downstream riparians.

If $3,000 is less than the cost to the polluter of
shutting down, or making the requisite tech-
nological changes, he might prefer to pay off the
damages (i.e., the legally cognizable damages)
and continue to pollute the stream. Similarly,
even if the court does issue an injunction at the
plaintiff's behest (rather than to order payment
of damages), there is nothing to stop the
plaintiffs from "selling out" the stream, i.e.,
agreeing with the polluter to dissolve or not
enforce the injunction at some price (in the example above, somewhere between plaintiffs'
damages—$3,000—and defendant's next best
economic alternative). Indeed, I take it this is
exactly what Learned Hand had in mind in an
opinion in which, after issuing an antipollution
injunction, he suggested that the defendant
"make its peace with the plaintiff as best it can."
What is meant is a peace—a deal—between
them, on their terms, and not between them and
the river.

I ought to make clear at this point that the
way the common law affects streams and rivers
is not exactly the same as the law affecting other
environmental objects. Indeed, one would be
hard pressed to say that there was a "typical"
environmental object, so far as the law is concerned. Differences exist in the law applicable
to rivers, lakes, oceans, dunes, air, streams (sur-
face and subterranean), beaches, and so forth.
And there is an even greater difference as be-

tween these traditional communal resources, on the one hand, and natural objects on land traditionally regarded as "private," e.g., the pond on the farmer's field, or the stand of trees on the suburbanite's lawn.

On the other hand, although these variances make it unwise to generalize about *a* law of the natural environment, none of the differences belie the points I have made. None of the natural objects, whether held in common or situated on private land, has any of the three criteria of a rights-holder under our legal system. They have no standing in their own right; their unique damages do not count in determining the outcome of a case; and they are not the beneficiaries of the law's awards. In such fashion, these objects have traditionally been regarded by the common law, and even by all but the most recent legislation, as objects for man to conquer and master and use—in such a way as the law once looked upon "man's" relationships to African Negroes. Even where special measures have been taken to conserve them, as by seasons on game and limits on timber cutting, the dominant concern has been to conserve them *for us*— i.e., only so far as inures to the greatest good of the greatest number of human beings. Conservationists, so far as I am aware, are generally reluctant to maintain otherwise. As the name implies, they want to conserve and guarantee our consumption and our enjoyment of these other living things. In their own right, natural objects have counted for little, in popular movements as in law.

⚜ TWO

Legal Rights for the Environment

As I stated at the outset, this rightlessness of the natural environment can and should change; it already shows some signs of doing so.

TOWARD HAVING STANDING IN ITS OWN RIGHT

It is not inevitable, nor is it wise, that natural objects should have no rights to seek redress in their own behalf. It is no answer to say that streams and forests cannot have standing because streams and forests cannot speak. Corporations, cannot speak either, nor can states, estates, infants, incompetents, municipalities or universities. Lawyers speak for them, as they customarily do for the ordinary citizen who has legal problems. One ought, I think, to handle the legal problems of natural objects as one does the problems of legal incompetents. If a human being shows signs of becoming senile and has affairs that he is not competent to manage, those concerned with his well-being make such a showing to the court, which can invest someone with the authority to manage the incompetent's affairs: a guardian (or "conservator" or "committee"—the terminology varies). Courts make similar arrangements when a corporation has become "incompetent"—they appoint a trustee in bankruptcy or reorganization to oversee its affairs and speak for it in court when that becomes necessary.

On a parity of reasoning, we should have a system in which, when a friend of a natural object perceives it to be endangered, he can apply to a court for the creation of a guardianship. Perhaps we already have the machinery to do so. California law, for example, defines an incompetent as:

> any person, whether insane or not, who by reason of old age, disease, weakness of mind, or other cause, is unable, unassisted, properly to manage and take care of himself or his property, and by reason thereof is likely to be deceived or imposed upon by artful or designing persons.

Are there not, among our natural objects, many such "persons" unable to take care of themselves—any number of rivers mutely choking to death—that need legal voice if they are not continuously to be "imposed upon"? To urge this upon a court calls for no more boldness or imagination than it took to convince the Supreme Court in the 1880s that a railroad was a "person" under the Fourteenth Amendment, a constitutional provision theretofore thought to secure the rights of freedmen, not corporate organizations. If such arguments based on a favorable interpretation of existing statutes should fail in the courts, special environmental legislation could readily be enacted along traditional guardianship lines. Provisions could be designed for guardianships both in the instance of public natural objects (e.g., rivers, beaches) and also, probably with slightly different standards, in the instance of natural objects on "private" land.*

* The law has developed in such a way that the private landowner's power over natural objects on his land is far less restrained by law (as opposed to the economics of self-interest) than his power over the public resources that he can get his hands on. If this state of affairs is to be changed, the standard for interceding in the interests of natural objects on traditionally recognized "private" land might well parallel the rules that guide courts in the matter of people's children whose upbringing (or lack thereof) poses social threat. The courts can, for example, make a child "a dependent of the court" where the child's "home is an unfit place for him by reason of neglect, cruelty, or depravity of either of his parents. . . ." California Welfare and

The potential "friends" that such a statutory scheme would require will hardly be lacking. The National Audubon Society, The Sierra Club, Environmental Defense Fund, Friends of the Earth, Natural Resources Defense Council, and the Izaak Walton League are just some of the many groups dedicated to environmental protection and which are becoming increasingly capable of marshaling the requisite technical experts and lawyers. If, for example, the Environmental Defense Fund should have reason to believe that some company's strip-mining operations were irreparably destroying the ecological balance of large tracts of land, it could, under this procedure, apply to the court in which the lands were situated to be appointed guardian. As guardian, it might be given rights of inspection (or visitation) to enter the property and bring to the court's attention details of the land's condition. If there were indications that under the substantive law some redress might be available on the land's behalf, then the guardian would be entitled to raise the land's rights in the land's name, i.e., without having to make the roundabout and often unavailing demonstration, discussed below, that "rights" of the club's members were being invaded. Guardians would also

Institutions Code § 600(b). That is to say, in extreme cases of child abuse, we intercede with the child's "owner"; surely there are extreme cases of environmental abuse where the society might feel it appropriate to intercede on behalf of an owner's natural objects.

be looked to for a host of other protective tasks, e.g., monitoring effluents (and/or monitoring the monitors), and representing their "wards" at legislative and administrative hearings on such matters as the setting of state water-quality standards. Procedures already exist, and can be strengthened, under which someone can move a court to remove and substitute guardians (for conflicts of interest or for other reasons) as well as to terminate the guardianship when the need has passed.

It is true there is a labyrinth of ontological problems we could become lost in here: which natural objects are we going to countenance as jural "persons"—the ecology of a bay? the oyster bed on its floor? each oyster? If a guardianship can be established over a forest, someone may ask, why not over an earthworm? Are we to concern ourselves with a watershed, a tributary, or a river? Suppose a guardian is appointed by a county court with respect to a stream, and a federal court appoints a guardian, with different ideas, for the larger river basin system of which the stream is a part.

One can spin off a myriad of complicated scenarios, all with an eye toward frightening the law away from the guardianship idea: court calendars clogged to a halt with trivia, endless jurisdictional disputes with the guardian for one entity setting himself at odds with the guardian for another, and the like. But to my mind, no one sympathetic to the environment should be put off because somewhere, far on the other side of this new legal territory, there may lie some mountains we don't know now how to cross. (They may be molehills when we get there.) Whatever hypotheticals we can conjure in the classroom, no lawyer I know in the real world is about to invest his time going to court to ask for a guardianship over an oyster or an earthworm. And I don't know any judge who would grant the motion if he or she did.*

But I do know at least one lawyer who is preparing papers on behalf of a stand of first-growth redwoods; another who has gone to bat, successfully to date, on behalf of a river; another—successfully, also—in the name of a commons.** I expect, in other words, that we are not as likely to suffer from a surfeit of trivial environmental representatives as we are to gain from new voices being heard in eminently sensible ones.

I am similarly inclined to discount some of

* Unless, perhaps, it were the last earthworm of a species, which most of us would regard as another matter. One ought to remember here, too, that we are speaking of the establishment of a guardianship as the first step in having a case presented on its merits. The granting of the guardianship merely ensures the natural object of its "day in court"—not a victory. The natural tendency is, that lawyers will not press for every imaginable guardianship, when the ward's chances of prevailing in the ultimate litigation are nil.

** These and similar cases are discussed below.

the potential jurisdictional problems. My guess is that the boundaries of the objects whose representation is sought will be determined, in the first instance, by the nature of the threat. If the threat is to a stream (and all that is involved in its present ecological balance), then the application for the guardianship will be made to the local court in whose jurisdiction the stream runs; the suit will be brought in the name of the stream, but the arguments advanced are not likely to be inconsistent with the interests of any component elements involved, i.e., the fish in the stream, the frogs on the banks, etc. Under most circumstances they will be suffering equally from the same complained-of actions. A whole watershed will be represented if it is the whole watershed that is being threatened, as by some lumbering or strip-mining operation. Something that threatened the entire atmosphere (the continued production of aerosol cans?) might lead to a guardianship on behalf of it, application to be made, perhaps, in a court of international jurisdiction.

In sum, I don't deny the many potential problems implicit in the idea I am putting forward; but most of them, I expect, we can deal with well enough when and if they really arise.

In point of fact, there already is a movement in the law toward giving the environment the benefits of standing—although not in a manner as satisfactory as the guardianship approach. There has been a marked liberalization of traditional standing requirements in recent cases in which environmental action groups have challenged federal government action. *Scenic Hudson Preservation Conference v. F.P.C.* is a good example of this development. There, the Federal Power Commission had granted New York's Consolidated Edison a license to construct a hydroelectric project on the Hudson River at Storm King Mountain. The grant of license had been opposed by conservation interests on the grounds that the transmission lines would be unsightly, fish would be destroyed, and nature trails would be inundated. Two of these conservation groups, united under the name Scenic Hudson Preservation Conference, petitioned the Second Circuit to set aside the grant. The F.P.C. responded that Scenic Hudson had no standing because it had not made the traditional claim of "personal economic injury resulting from the Commission's actions." Nonetheless, the court decided to hear the petitions and sent the case back to the Commission for further findings on environmental injury. On the standing point, the court noted that Section 313 (b) of the Federal Power Act gave a right of instituting a review to any party "aggrieved by an order issued by the Commission"; obviously prompted by some solicitude for the environment, and desirous that someone be available to plead the environment's cause, the court thereupon read "aggrieved by" as not limiting suit to those suffering the personal economic injury required by traditional law. The statutory language, the court said, was broad enough to allow standing for "those who by their acitivities and conduct have exhibited a special interest" in "the aesthetic, conservational and recreational aspect of power development. . . ." A similar reasoning has swayed other circuits to allow challenges to the Federal Power Commission, the Department of the Interior, and the Department of Health, Education and Welfare, on the theory that contemplated actions injurious to the environment "injured" the recreational and esthetic interests of environmental group members.

Then, in 1970, the United States Court of Appeals for the Ninth Circuit cast a shadow over this trend towards liberalized standing. The case grew out of an application by Walt Disney Enterprises to construct a $35,000,000 complex of motels, restaurants and recreational facilities in Mineral King Valley, a wilderness area in California's Sierra Nevada Mountains. The Department of the Interior, which has jurisdiction over the area (through the U.S. Forest Service), granted Disney a permit. But the Sierra Club, which had been strongly opposed to the "development", won a preliminary injunction in the U.S. District Court. On Disney's appeal, however, the Ninth Circuit reasoned that the Sierra Club "does not allege that it is aggrieved" or that it is "adversely affected within the meaning of the rules of standing. . . . The right to sue does not inure to one who does not possess it, simply because there is no one else willing and able to assert it."

It was almost immediately after this decision that I wrote the article from which this book has been drawn. Perhaps injury to the Sierra Club was tenuous, but "injury" to the park itself would be easier to demonstrate. Thus, I felt, if I could get the courts to conceive Mineral King Valley as itself a party in the eyes of the law, it would be easier to prove the injury on which standing would seemingly have to depend: injury to the plaintiff itself.

On appeal to the United States Supreme Court, the Sierra Club lost. Justice Potter Stewart, writing for the four-man majority (two recent appointees did not participate in the judgment), declared that "a mere 'interest in a problem,' no matter how long-standing the interest and no matter how qualified the organization is in evaluating the problem, is not sufficient to render the organization 'adversely affected' or 'aggrieved' within the meaning of the [Administrative Procedure Act]." "The 'injury in fact' test," the Court went on to say, "requires more than an injury to a cognizeable interest. It requires that the party seeking review be himself among the injured."

Did this mean that the Sierra Club (or its individual members) were not, in the Court's eyes, "among the injured"? The answer was not left clear. Interpreting the Sierra Club's complaint somewhat narrowly, Stewart said that

49

"the Sierra Club *failed to allege* [emphasis added] that it or its members would be affected in any of their activities or pastimes by the Disney development." The majority opinion then proceeded, in a footnote, to hint that: "Our decision does not, of course, bar the Sierra Club from seeking in the District Court to amend its complaint by a motion under Rule 15, Federal Rules of Civil Procedure." In other words, as a matter of judicial protocol, the Court would not commit itself to say in advance what allegations, exactly, would satisfy the standing requirement—it would say little more than that, whatever the Sierra Club had pleaded thus far, wasn't enough.

Justices William O. Douglas, Harry A. Blackmun, and William O. Brennan dissented, each of them taking the position that the case should have been heard on the merits, then and there. On the standing point, Justice Douglas began by endorsing my thesis, then recently published in the U.S.C. Law Review (too late, of course, for it to have been incorporated in the pleadings). "The critical question of 'standing'," he wrote,

> would be simplified and also put neatly in focus if we fashioned a federal rule that allowed environmental issues to be litigated before federal agencies or federal courts in the name of the inanimate object about to be despoiled, defaced, or invaded. . . . Contemporary public concern for protecting

nature's ecological equilibrium should lead to the conferral of standing upon environmental objects to sue for their own preservation. See Stone, *Should Trees Have Standing? Toward Legal Rights for Natural Objects*, 45 S. Cal. L. Rev. 450 (1972). This suit would therefore be more properly labeled as *Mineral King v. Morton*.

Justice Blackmun, the Nixon appointee who had heretofore been in accord with Justice Douglas only rarely, agreed, adding for his part that Justice Douglas's "eloquent opinion has imaginatively suggested another means [to locate standing] and one, in its own way, with obvious, appropriate and self-imposed limitations."

To the date of this writing, this remains the last, indecisive word we have had from the United States Supreme Court. Three Justices, apparently, seem prepared to accept some legal claims in the name of the natural object itself. Two justices did not participate; and four chose not to respond to my theory, it not having, technically speaking, been raised.

These same four judges—the majority—did, however, leave open a possibility that they might be satisfied with a repleading by the Sierra Club that clarified and emphasized reasons for standing in the club's own name, and/or particularized some grievances of one or more of the club's members. The Sierra Club subsequently decided to take this tack in its amended

51

complaint, which is now (March 1975) docketed in the United States District Court for the
Northern District of California.

Even if the Sierra Club should be able to sustain its modified pleading through the courts,
and keep so-called "liberalized standing" alive,
there are significant reasons to continue pressing
for the guardianship approach as an alternate or
even supplemental basis for standing. For one
thing, successful cases of the liberalized standing sort must be rested on interpretations of particular federal statutes—the Federal Power
Commission Act, the Administrative Procedure
Act, the Federal Insecticide, Fungicide and Rodenticide Act, and others. Thus, this avenue will
support environmental suits *only when the environment is threatened by acts of federal
agencies;* and even in those areas, it will work
only when a relevant law contains some special
standing provision which can be interpreted to
free the courts from their traditional restrictions.
(The Ninth Circuit has clearly intimated as
much.) The fate of pro-environmental cases
where there is not such special statutory provision is indicated in *Bass Angler Sportsman
Society v. United States Steel Corp.* There,
plaintiffs sued 175 corporate defendants located
throughout Alabama, relying on a clause of the
Federal River and Harbor Act which provides:

It shall not be lawful to throw, discharge,
or deposit . . . any refuse matter . . . into

any navigable water of the United States,
or into any tributary of any navigable water
from which the same shall float or be
washed into such navigable water. . . .

Ordinarily, only the government has standing
to enforce such a federal criminal provision. But
the government had refused (in the face of considerable evidence of pollution) to take on the
corporations. To support its own right to bring
the suit, the plaintiffs pointed to another, rather
unusual section of the Act, which provides that
one-half the fines shall be paid to the person or
persons giving information which shall lead to a
conviction. Claiming this latter provision could
be interpreted as an indirect basis for investing
them with standing to sue, the plaintiffs desig-
nated their action a *qui tam* action (an old form
of action brought by a citizen on behalf of the
state as well as for himself) and sought to enforce the Act themselves by injunction and fine. It
was not an implausible position. But the District
Court ruled that, in the absence of the most express language to the contrary, no one outside
the Department of Justice had standing to sue
under a criminal act and refused to reach the
question of whether violations were occurring.
Other attempted *qui tam* actions brought by the
Bass Angler Sportsman Society in other states
have been similarly unsuccessful.

There are, in sum, reasons to believe that the
liberalized standing approach has not the poten-

53

tial of the guardianship approach to secure an effective voice for the environment where federal administrative action and public lands are not involved. But most important of all, whatever the ultimate fate of the Sierra Club's conservative repleading in the Mineral King matter, I doubt that the liberalized standing concept is going to have continued viability; it is only a matter of time before the courts realize that, as a matter of judicial economy, it will prove simply unmanageable. The seeds of its self-destruction are this: if any group can get into court simply by pleading an injury as ephemeral as the aesthetic and recreational interests of its members, how can the flow of litigation be controlled? Granted, just allowing suits on behalf of the environment—my proposal—poses an increased burden on the courts. But to allow just about anyone a right to sue on behalf of just about everything, without the traditional gatecheck of real economic injury, would be a judicial nightmare. If an ad hoc Committee to Protect the Forest loses its suit, what happens when its very same members reorganize ten months later and sue under the name of Committee to Preserve Our Trees? Is the new group to be bound by the earlier decision (what lawyers call *res judicata*)? The "new group" now says it has discovered a slightly different rationale; the "other group" was relying on a forester, but the "new group" says it is going to put biologists on the stand. The "other group" was focusing on the problem from the point of view of lost hiking trials, but the new group is coming at the problem now as frustrated canoeists.

Class-action law may be capable of heading off some of the more blatant duplications. But even so, it makes more practical sense to designate some particular guardian *the* legal representative of the natural object, and have the suit brought in the name of the object. This heads off somewhat the threat of duplicated suits, by making it clear that the natural object—treated as the party in interest—is "bound" by an adverse judgment. Further, the hearing on the selection of the guardian gives some assurance that the environment will be represented by the most effective voice available. These are the sorts of considerations Justice Blackmun was hinting at when he observed that the guardianship proposal was not merely imaginative, but that it had "in its own way ... obvious, appropriate and self-imposed limitations."

This, while it may sound odd and fanciful, when you get right down to it, the guardianship concept makes more sense than the alternatives. It would provide the endangered natural object with what the trustee in bankruptcy provides the endangered corporation: a continuous responsibility and supervision over a period of time, with a consequent deeper understanding of a broad range of the ward's problems, not just the problems present in one particular piece of litigation. It would help assure the courts that when a lawsuit is brought on behalf of the environment, the object will be represented not by some casual romantic, but by someone with the expertise and genuine interest in pressing the claim which are the prerequisites of a true "case or controversy."

There are two objections that can be raised against the guardianship approach, neither of which seems to me persuasive, however. The first is that it would be impossible for the guardian to judge the needs of the river or forest in its charge; indeed, the very concept of "needs," it might be said, could be used here only in the most metaphorical way. The second objection is that such a system would not be much different from what we now have: is not the Department of the Interior already such a guardian for public lands, and do not most states have legislation empowering their attorneys general to seek relief (on a sort of *parens patriae* basis) for the very sort of injuries our guardian is to concern himself with?

As for the first objection, I think it is too easy to overstate the problem. Natural objects *can* communicate their wants (needs) to us, and in ways that are not terribly ambiguous. I am sure I can judge with as much certainty and meaningfulness whether and when my lawn wants (needs) water, as the Attorney General can judge whether and when the United States wants (needs) to take an appeal from an adverse judgment by a lower court. The lawn tells me that it wants water by a certain dryness of the blades and soil—immediately obvious to the touch—the appearance of bald spots, yellowing, and a lack of springiness after being walked on; how does "the United States" communicate to the Attorney General? For similar reasons, the guardian-attorney for a smog-endangered stand of pines could venture with more confidence that his client wants the smog stopped than the directors of a corporation can assert that "the corporation" wants dividends declared. We make decisions on behalf of, and in the purported interests of, others every day. These "others" are often creatures whose wants are far less verifiable, and even far more metaphysical in conception, than the wants of rivers, trees, and land.*

---

* But here, as in other aspects of incorporating natural objects into the legal system, we are dogged by the ontological problem I referred to earlier. It is easier to venture that the smog-endangered stand of pines "wants" the smog stopped (assuming that to be the jurally significant entity) then it is to venture that the mountain, or the planet earth, or the cosmos, is concerned about whether the pines stand or fall. The more encompassing the entity of concern, the less certain we can be in venturing judgments as to the "wants" of any particular substance, quality, or species within the universe. Does the cosmos care if we humans persist or not? "Heaven and earth . . . regard all things as insignificant, as though they were playthings made of straw." Lao-Tzu, *Tao Teh King*. The notion of needs is thus tied in with our notions of what objects are *significant*; these notions, in turn, are not static. They will shift as our own intel-

As for the second objection, there is, it is true, historical evidence that the Department of the Interior was conceived as a sort of guardian of the public lands. But there are several points that undermine the suggestion that our guardian would merely duplicate the function of the Interior. First, insofar as the department already is an adequate guardian, it is only with respect to the *federal public lands* (as provided in Article IV of the Constitution). Its guardianship includes neither local public lands nor private lands. Second, to judge from the environmentalist literature and from the cases environmental action groups have been bringing, the department is itself one of the bogeys of the environmental movement. (One thinks of the uneasy peace between the Indians and the Bureau of Indian Affairs.) Whether the various charges be right or wrong, one cannot help but observe that the department has been charged with several institutional goals (never an easy burden), and is under the constant stress of inconsistent pressures from quite a variety of conflicting interest groups, only one of which is the environmentalists. In this context, having a guardian independent of the established institutional framework becomes especially valuable. Besides, what a person wants, fully to secure his rights, is the ability to retain independent coun-

---

lectual—including aesthetic and moral—appreciation and consciousness develop. This interrelationship is discussed in Chapter 4.

sel even when, and perhaps especially when, the government is acting "for him" in a beneficent way. I have no reason to doubt, for example, that the Social Security System is being managed "for me"; but I would not want to abdicate my right to challenge its actions as they affect me, should the need arise. I would not ask more trust of national forests, vis-à-vis the Department of the Interior. The same considerations apply in the instance of local agencies, such as regional water-pollution boards, whose members' expertise in pollution matters often comes (as in California) from their being dominated by representatives of the very industries that are doing the polluting. There is no real substitute for independent environmental counsel being available when the need arises.

The objection that attorneys-general are already available as protectors of the environment is answerable in much the same manner. Their authority to intervene on behalf of the environment is narrowly circumscribed and often uncertain. As political creatures, attorneys general must tread softly, exercising whatever powers they might have with "discretion." Indeed, one has only to look to the present state of the environment, and the cautious application and development of environmental protection laws long on the books (the Federal River and Harbor Act is over seventy years old) to see that the many diverse burdens of being an attorney general don't leave much time for the protection of nature. No doubt, a strengthening public interest in the environment—if it can sustain itself through the energy crunch—will increase the zest of public attorneys even where, as will often be the case, well-represented corporations must be their quarry. Indeed, there are signs recent United States Attorneys General have stepped up antipollution enforcement, and they ought to be further encouraged in this direction. Their statutory powers should be enlarged, and they should be armed with criminal penalties made at least commensurate with the likely economic benefits of violating the law.*

On the other hand, one cannot ignore the fact that there is increased pressure on public law-enforcement officers to give more attention to a host of other problems, from crime "in the streets" (why don't we say "in the rivers"?) to

---

* To be really effective as a deterrent, the law's sanctions must be made high enough that the corporation will feel it, and institute the requisite reorganization of its internal structure: appropriate changes in the company's production methods, quality control, patterns of authority, etc. Otherwise, they will simply absorb the fine as a mere "cost of doing business" and continue taking high risks of repeated violations. Because the corporation is not necessarily a profit-maximizing "rationally economic man," there is no reason to believe that setting the fine as high as—but no higher than—anticipated profits from the violation of the law, will be adequate to overcome the corporate inertia against changed ways of doing things. This problem, and what we have to do about it, is dealt with in my book, *Where the Law Ends: The Social Control of Corporate Behavior* (Harper & Row 1975).

consumerism, school busing, and energy. If the environment is not to get lost in the shuffle, we would do well to adopt the guardianship approach as an additional safeguard, conceptualizing major natural objects as holders of their own rights, raisable on their behalf by the court-appointed guardian.

TOWARD RECOGNITION OF
ITS OWN INJURIES

Thus far I have been arguing for environmental standing—for getting the environment its "day in court." Let me turn now to the second feature of being a holder of rights: we have to arrange for a judicial accounting of harm to the environment—in its own right.

As indicated above, the traditional way of deciding whether to issue injunctions in lawsuits affecting the environment, at least where communal property is involved, has been to strike some sort of balance regarding the economic hardships on competing human interests, not among the human interests and the environment. Even Justice Douglas, our jurist most closely associated with conservation sympathies, was recently deciding the propriety of a new dam on the basis of, among other things, anticipated lost profits from fish catches, some $12,-

000,000 annually. Although he decided to delay the project involved pending further findings, the reasoning seems unnecessarily incomplete and compromising. Why should the environment be of importance only indirectly, as lost profits to someone else? Why not throw into the balance the cost to the environment?

The case for "personifying" the environment in this second sense—of making a separate accounting of its own legal damages—is a corollary of a fundamental assumption of welfare economics. Every well-working legal-economic system should be so arranged as to confront each of us with the full costs that our activities are imposing on society. Ideally, a paper mill, in deciding what to produce—and where, and by what methods—ought to be forced to take into account not only the lumber, acid, and labor that its production "takes" from other uses in the society (which is thereby a "cost" to the rest of us), but also those costs it imposes through pollution. The legal system, through the law of contracts and the criminal law, makes the mill absorb—and thus really consider—the first group of its demands. When, for example, the company's purchasing agent orders 1,000 drums of acid from the Z Company, the Z Company can bind the mill to pay for them; in this way the mill reimburses the society for what it is removing from alternative uses to which the acid might have been put by someone else. And the law thereby guarantees that the mill will not be ill-considered and lavish with its factors of production: it has to pay for what it takes.

But unfortunately, so far as pollution and other environmental costs are concerned, this ideal of pay-for-what-you-take begins to break down: the law has a more difficult time "catching" and confronting the polluting corporations with the full social costs of the harms they are causing. In the lakeside mill example, major riparian interests might possibly bring pollution suits, so that a court will weigh their aggregate losses against the costs to the mill of installing a good antipollution system. But many other interests—and I am speaking for the moment even of traditionally recognized human interests—are too fragmented and perhaps "too remote" causually to warrant their securing representation and pressing for recovery: the people who own summer homes and motels, the man who sells fishing tackle and bait, the man who rents rowboats. These damage claims may represent, in the aggregate, a considerable amount of social loss. But under our present system, the law may never arrange for them to be borne by the responsible actor for any of a number of technical, as well as practical reasons. For example, the United States Supreme Court, in *Eisen v. Carlisle & Jacquelin,* ruled in 1974 that anyone who wants to start a class action has to bear the expense of locating and notifying each and every member of the class, even if no single prospective class member (injured party) has a large enough stake in the matter to justify separate litigation of his individual claim.

Consider in this context, too, another of the Court's 1974 decisions, *Zahn v. International Paper Co. Zahn* arose out of allegations that International Paper Company was permitting discharge from one of its New York pulp and paper-making plants to flow into Ticonderoga Creek and to be carried by that stream into Lake Champlain, thereby polluting the lake's waters and damaging the value of the lakeside properties. A group of lakefront owners brought a federal court action against the corporation for damages—a class action on behalf of themselves and two hundred owners and lessees of property that surrounded the lake. Their suit ran aground because to get into federal court in an action of this sort, a plaintiff has to be able to allege damages of $10,000 as a minimum jurisdictional amount. While some of the plaintiffs may have suffered $10,000 damages, the District Court was convinced "to a legal certainty" that not every individual owner in the class had suffered pollution damages in that amount, and went on to rule that in those circumstances, even though the total suit involved over $10,000, the fact that each and every party in the class had not suffered the jurisdictional minimum blocked the whole suit from proceeding. The opinion was upheld by a divided Court of Appeals, and then, once more, by a divided United States Supreme Court.

To meet problems such as these, doesn't it make better sense to constitute the lake a party to the lawsuit, allowing it, through its guardian, to prove the damages to these fragmented human interests as the prima facie measure of damages to it, which *it* ought to recover? By doing so, we in effect make the natural object, through its guardian, a jural entity competent to gather up these otherwise unrepresented damage claims, and press them before the court even where, for legal or practical reasons, they are not going to be pressed by traditional class action plaintiffs. Indeed, one way—the anthropocentric way—to view my proposal so far, is to view the guardian of the natural object as the guardian of unborn generations, as well as of the otherwise unrepresented, but distantly injured, contemporary humans. By making the lake itself the focus of these damages, and "incorporating" it, so to speak, the legal system can effectively take proof upon, and confront the polluter with, a larger and more representative measure of the damages its pollution is causing than is possible under the law as it now stands.*

With what I have been saying so far, my economist friends (unremittent human chauvinists, every one of them!) have no large quarrel in principle. The proposal can be viewed as a legalistic *trompe l'oeil* that, if it works, simply

* Later, if some of the minor human interests did want to call upon their share of the recovery, a distribution from the lake's fund could easily be arranged.

effectuates the goals of the ideal class action, or the ideal water-pollution control district. This is where we are apt to part company: I propose going beyond gathering up the loose ends of what almost all of us recognize as legitimate, traditional damage claims. I favor a system in which the guardian would urge before the court injuries not presently cognizable—the death of eagles and inedible crabs, the suffering of sea lions, the loss from the face of the earth of species of commercially valueless birds, the disappearance of a wilderness area. One might, of course, speak of the damages involved as "damages" to us humans in a derivative way; the widespread growth of environmental groups testifies to how many humans feel these losses. But feelings are hard to measure; and how can we impute to these "worthless" claims a monetary value which the guardian can raise in court?

We have to begin by recognizing that the law is no stranger to the complex process of *creating monetary worth*. Wherever the law chooses to assign "property" rights—and thus lend certain claims the mantle of its protection—it puts the value of something on a solid foundation. One's literary works would have minimal monetary value if anyone could copy them at will. Their economic value to the author is a product of the law of copyright; the copyright has value because the law *says* whoever holds it can demand a fee from whoever copies the work. Similarly, it is through the law of torts that we have made a "right" of—and guaranteed an economically meaningful value to—privacy. The notion of a property right in one's privacy barely existed before it was "invented" in an 1898 Harvard Law Review article by young Louis Brandeis and his then law partner, Charles Warren. They convinced the law to make it so. The value we place on gold—a yellow inanimate dirt—is not simply a function of supply and demand (wilderness areas are scarce and pretty, too), but is connected with the actions of the legal systems of the world, which have institutionalized that value. I am proposing we do the same with eagles and wilderness areas as we do with copyrighted works, patented inventions, and privacy: make the violation of rights in them to be a cost by declaring the "pirating" of them to be the invasion of a property interest. If we do so, the net social costs the polluter would be confronted with would include not only the extended anthropocentric costs of his pollution (explained above) but also costs to the environment per se.

This, though, only says that we could declare various environmental objects have value *in principle*. It leaves open the problem, if damages are to be imposed on someone who has intruded upon these values, how are the costs—the actual monetary worth—to be calculated? When we protect (give property rights in) an invention, there is at least a basis in market demand for it, by reference to which damages against a patent infringer can be computed. But the lost environmental "values" of which we are now speaking lie outside what any market is prepared to bid for: they are, in this peculiar sense, priceless.

One possible measure of damages, suggested earlier, would be to assess the wrongdoer the cost of making the environment whole; i.e., putting it in the position it was in (would have been in) had the wrongful injuries not occurred. When a man is injured in an automobile accident, for example, we impose upon the responsible party the injured man's medical expenses and lost salary. A comparable award to a polluted river would include the costs of dredging, restocking with fish, and so forth. It is on the basis of such costs as these, I assume, that we get the figure of $1,000,000,000 as the cost of saving Lake Erie. As an ideal, I think this is a guideline applicable in many environmental situations. It is by no means free from difficulties, however.

One problem with computing damages on the basis of making the environment whole is that, if recoveries on behalf of natural objects were awarded consistently, it would bring us close to asking for a "freeze" on present environmental quality, even at the costs (and there will be costs) of preserving "useless" objects.* The vir-

* One ought to observe, too, that in terms of real effects on marginal welfare, it is certainly the poor who are most unfairly burdened by compromises in favor of the environment. It is they, on the one hand, who are

tues of such a possible "freeze" should not be rejected out of hand, especially when we consider that, even by reference to the most immediately discernible homocentric interests, there are so many areas in which we ought to be cleaning up and not merely preserving the environmental status quo. In fact, the Congress has demanded, over a presidential veto, that there be a total elimination of all river pollutants by 1985, notwithstanding that such a decision would impose quite large direct and indirect costs on us all. Here one is inclined to recall the instructions of Judge Hays, in remanding Consolidated Edison's Storm King application to the Federal Power Commission in *Scenic Hudson*:

> The Commission's renewed proceedings must include as a basic concern the preservation of natural beauty and of natural historic shrines, keeping in mind that, in our affluent society, the cost of a project [meaning the cost "to people"] is only one of several factors to be considered.

Nevertheless, whatever the merits of "total purity" as an ideal, the social price tag of putting it into effect will often be too high to accept. Consider, for example, an oceanside nu-

the most pinched when an environmentalist victory forces a utility to raise its rates; they, too, most lack the wherewithal to take their families camping to enjoy the scene of the victory.

clear generator that could produce low-cost electricity for a million homes at a savings of $1 a year per home, spare us the air pollution that comes of burning fossil fuels, but which through a slight heating effect threatened to kill off a rare species of temperature-sensitive sea urchins; suppose, further, that technological improvements adequate to reduce the temperature to present environmental quality would expend the entire $1,000,000 in anticipated fuel savings. Are we prepared to tax ourselves $1,000,000 a year on behalf of the sea urchins? In comparable problems under the present law we work out practicable compromises by abandoning *restoration costs* as the measure of damages and calling upon *fair market value*. For example, if an automobile is so severely damaged that the cost of repairing it (making it "whole") is greater than its fair market value, we allow the party responsible for the accident to pay the fair market value only. Or if a human being suffers the loss of an arm (compare the ocean having irreparably lost the sea urchins), we can capitalize his reduced earning power (and pain and suffering) to measure the damages. But what is the fair market value of sea urchins? How can we capitalize their loss to the ocean, independent of any commercial value they have to someone else?

One answer is that the problem can sometimes be sidestepped quite satisfactorily. In the sea urchin example, one compromise solution would be to impose on the nuclear generator the costs of making the ocean whole somewhere else, in some other way, e.g., reestablishing a sea urchin colony elsewhere, or making a somehow comparable contribution. In the debate over the laying of the trans-Alaskan pipeline, the builders proposed at one point to meet conservationists' objections halfway by reestablishing wildlife away from the pipeline, so far as is feasible.

But even if damage calculations have to be made, one ought to recognize that the measurement of damages is rarely a simple report of economic facts about "the market," whether we are valuing the loss of a foot, a fetus, or a work of fine art. Courts have not been reluctant to award damages for the destruction of heirlooms, literary manuscripts, or other property having no ascertainable market value. Decisions of this sort are always hard, but not impossible. We have increasingly taken (human) pain and suffering into account in reckoning damages, not because anyone believes we can place an "objective" value on them, but because, even in view of all the room for disagreement, we come up with a better society by making rude estimates than by ignoring them altogether. We can make such estimates in regard to environmental losses fully aware that what we are really doing is making implicit normative judgments (as with pain and suffering)—laying down rules that as much declare what the society is going to "value" as report it. In making such estimates, decision makers would not go wrong if they estimated on the "high side," putting the burden of trimming the figure down on the adverse human interests. All burdens of proof should reflect common experience; and our experience in environmental matters has generally been that each earlier injury to the environment has wound up causing more long-range damage than anyone had been able to appreciate at the time.

To what extent the decision maker should factor in costs such as the pain and suffering of animals and other sentient natural objects, I cannot say; although I am prepared to do so in principle. (It is not easy to dismiss the idea of even "lower" life—plants and similar objects—having consciousness and feeling pain, especially since it is so difficult to know what these terms mean even as applied to humans.) But it seems to me that the resulting damages would turn out to be so marginal, and our estimates in this area need be so conjectural and approximate in all events, that admitting such a practice would be more significant theoretically than from any changes it would work in the operation of the legal system.

TOWARD BEING A BENEFICIARY IN
ITS OWN RIGHT

As suggested above, one reason for making the environment the beneficiary of a judgment in its own right is to prevent it from being "sold out" in a negotiation among private litigants: should a decree enjoining despoilation be entered between human interests alone, there is nothing to prevent the victor from agreeing—at a price—not to enforce his legal rights. The natural object can be protected from this possibility only if it itself is made a party to the injunctive settlement.

Even more importantly, we should make it possible for the natural object itself to be a beneficiary of money awards. If, in making the balance of interests requisite to issuing an injunction, a court decides not to enjoin a lake polluter who is causing injury to the extent of $50,000 annually, but to have the polluter pay damages instead, then the lake ought to be entitled to its share, along with the riparian humans who are going to have to suffer. The natural object's portion should be put into a trust fund to be administered by the object's guardian, as per the guardianship proposal set forth above. Guardians' fees, including legal fees, would then come out of this fund. More importantly, the guardian would draw on the available monies to preserve the natural object as much as possible—purchasing new stock, installing aeration systems, or doing whatever seemed most appropriate.

The idea of assessing damages as best we can and placing them in a trust fund is far more realistic than a hope that a total "freeze" can be put on the environmental status quo. Nature is a continuous theater in which things and species (eventually man) are destined to enter and exit. In the meantime, coexistence of man and his environment means that each is going to have to compromise for the better of both. Some pollution of streams, for example, will probably be inevitable for a long time. Instead of pretending to set an unrealizable goal—enjoining absolutely the discharge of all such pollutants—the trust fund concept would (a) help assure that pollution would occur only in those instances where the social need for the polluter's product (via his present method of production) was so great as to enable the polluter to cover all homocentric costs, *plus* some estimated costs to the environment per se, and (b) would, if necessary, be a corpus for preserving monies while the technology developed to a point where repairing the damaged portion of the environment became feasible. Such a fund might even be used to finance the requisite ecological and technical research and development.

THREE

Toward Substantive
Rights for the Environment

So far we have looked at what is involved, in general, in being a holder of rights, and examined some of the implications that making the environment a holder of rights would entail. Natural objects would have standing in their own right, to be asserted by a guardian; their own damages would be ascertained as an independent factor in weighing judicial relief; and they would be the recipients of legal awards for their own benefit. But these considerations give us only the skeleton of what would be involved. To flesh out the "rights" of the environment demands that we provide it with a significant and more detailed body of rules to deal with its claims when it gets to court.

What would such a body of rules look like? To say that natural objects should have rights does not settle what rights they should have.

But nor does saying the law "should be conducive to the greatest good of the greatest number [of people]" yield answers to specific questions. Principles on this level of generality are statements *about* a legal system, not *of* them; their function is to give guidance to the lawmakers, on whose shoulders falls the task of translating the principle (the greatest good of the greatest number) into actual practices (should adopted children have the right to learn the identity of their biological parents?). This task, in turn, is a never-ending one, a laboratory experiment for which there are, in fact, no ultimate solutions. Thus, we cannot produce here and now a full-blown body of rules that engenders the principle of environmental rights-holding. But there are some important observations to be made about what this body of rules would involve.

To begin with, the lawyer is constantly aware that a right is not, as the layman may think, a concrete entity that one either has or has not. One's life, one's right to vote, one's property, can all be taken away. But those who would infringe on them must go through certain procedures before they can do so. These procedures, in turn, are a measure of what we value as a society. Some of the most important questions of "right" thus turn into questions of procedure and degree: how much review, and of what sort, will which agencies of state accord us when we claim our "right" is being infringed? Where will the burden of proof lie? What sorts of evidence will be considered probative of sustaining a particular claim?

We do not have an absolute right either to our lives or to our driver's licenses. But we have a greater right to our lives because before we can be deprived of them—executed—there are more institutional barriers on our behalf, all to the effect that the state first make a very strong showing of cause. A single clerk in the Department of Motor Vehicles will not suffice; for our lives, the state will have to justify its actions before a grand jury, petit jury (convincing them "beyond a reasonable doubt"), sentencing jury, and, most likely, several levels of appellate courts. The carving out of students' "rights" to their education is being made up of this sort of procedural fabric. No one, I think, is maintaining that in no circumstances ought a student to be expelled from school. The battle for student "rights" involves shifting the answers to questions like these: before a student is expelled, does he have to be given a hearing; does he have to have prior notice of the hearing, and notice of charges; may he bring counsel, (need the state provide a lawyer if he cannot?); need there be a transcript; need the school carry the burden of proving the charges; may he confront witnesses; if he is expelled, can he get review by a civil court; if he can get such review, need the school show its

77

actions were "reasonable," or merely "not unreasonable," and so forth?

In this vein, to bring the environment into the society as a rights-holder would not stand it on a better footing than the rest of us mere mortals, who every day must suffer some of the irreducible injuries of an overcrowded planet: a certain amount of smog, of noise, of limited space. Much of this sort of thing the law must write off as *damnum absque injuria*—harms for which there ultimately can be no redress. Forests are going to be cut, and fish fished.

The environment must look for its interest to be taken into account not through absolute bans on all incursions, but in subtler, more procedural ways.

The National Environmental Policy Act is a splendid example of this sort of rights-making through the elaboration of procedural safeguards. Among its many provisions, it establishes that every federal agency must:

> Include in every recommendation or report on proposals for legislation and other major federal actions significantly affecting the quality of the human environment, a detailed statement by the responsible official on—
> (i)   the environmental impact of the proposed action,
> (ii) any adverse environmental effects which

cannot be avoided should the proposal be implemented,

(iii) alternatives to the proposed action,

(iv) the relationship between local short-term uses of man's environment and the maintenance and enhancement of long-term productivity, and

(v) any irreversible and irretrievable commitments of resources which would be involved in the proposed action should it be implemented.

Prior to making any detailed statement, the responsible federal official must consult with and obtain the comments of any federal agency which has jurisdiction by law or special expertise with respect to any environmental impact involved. Copies of the statement and the comments and views of the appropriate federal, state, and local agencies, which are authorized to develop and enforce environmental standards, have to be made available to the President, the Council on Environmental Quality, and to the public, and are to accompany the proposal through the existing agency review processes.

Beyond this, the agency is instructed to "study, develop, and describe appropriate alternatives to recommend courses of action in any proposal which involves unresolved conflicts concerning alternative uses of available resources."

These procedural protections have already begun paying off in the courts. For example, it was on the basis of the Federal Power Commission's failure to make adequate inquiry into "alternatives" (as per subsection (iii)) in the *Scenic Hudson* case, above, and the Atomic Energy Commission's failure to make adequate findings, apparently as per subsections (i) and (ii), in connection with the Amchitka Island underground test explosion, that federal courts delayed the implementation of environment-threatening schemes.

Although this sort of control (remanding a cause to an agency for further findings) may seem to the layman ineffectual, or only a stalling of the inevitable, the lawyer and the organization analyst know that these demands for further findings can make a difference. It may encourage the institution whose actions threaten the environment to really *think about* what it is doing, and that is neither an ineffectual nor a small feat.

Let me give an example of how such "finding" requirements may combine, at their best. In early 1973, Orange County, New Jersey, was planning to build a new sewage treatment system. The *Wall Street Journal* reported:

> Questions were immediately raised. How would the new facility affect the aquatic life in the County's numerous lakes and streams? What would be the effect on veg-

etation that laces the County's miles of marshlands? What about animals? Houses? Local landmarks?

The story noted that only a few years ago such questions would probably have received "cursory consideration and prompt dismissal." But under the NEPA provisions it was necessary for the county to prepare and file an impact statement. The county officials, pursuant to the requirements, brought in a fisheries biologist, a terrestrial plant ecologist, and other various scientists to examine the scene. The results, according to the *Journal*, included:

- certain of the County's marshes, discovered to be a major source for many fish species and much of the County's wildlife, were set aside as untouchable by the projects;
- siltation of an important lake was prevented;
- a 250-year-old house and a 150-year-old mulberry tree, both popular with local residents, were rescued from the bulldozer;
- the sewage authority, because of these and other changes recommended in the impact statement . . . found that its project would cost some $700,000 less than had been originally estimated.

Indeed, I think such requirements are promising enough that I would extend them beyond governmental agencies. Much of the environment is threatened not by them, but by corporations —our private governments. Surely the constitutional power would not be lacking to require all corporations whose actions may have significant adverse affect on the environment to make findings of the sort now mandated for federal agencies. Further, there should be requirements to prevent these findings and reports from languishing in the files of lower-level management. Provisions can be drafted to assure that this information is channeled to the board of directors or other top policy makers, thereby charging them with the knowledge of what their corporation is doing to the environment. We might make it grounds for a guardian to enjoin a private corporation's actions if such internal information procedures had not been carried out.

The rights of the environment could be enlarged by borrowing yet another page from the Environmental Protection Act and establishing comparable provisions for the private sector. The Act sets up within the Executive Office of the President a Council on Environmental Quality "to be conscious of and responsive to the scientific, economic, social, esthetic, and cultural needs of the Nation; and to formulate and recommend policies to promote the improvement of the quality of the environment." The Council is to become a focal point, within our biggest "corporation"—the State—to gather and evaluate environmental information which it is to pass on to our chief executive officer, the President. Rather than being ineffectual, this may be a highly sophisticated way of steering organizational behavior. As I explain more fully in *Where the Law Ends*, corporations in many industries—especially recidivist polluters and land despoilers —should have to establish a comparable internal organization, e.g., to set up a Vice-President for Ecological Affairs, and make him personally responsible for overseeing the organizational structure, information flow, etc. necessary to protect the environment's interests. I am not offering the suggestion as a cure-all, by any means, but this sort of control over internal corporate organization would be an effective supplement to the traditional mechanisms of civil suits, licensing, administrative agencies, and fines as a way of increasing the environment's rights.

Similarly, courts should be compelled in appropriate cases to make findings with respect to environmental harm—showing how they calculated the damages and how heavily it was weighed—even in matters that lie outside the present Environmental Protection Act, and perhaps even where the environment is not, strictly speaking, a party. This would have at least two important consequences: first, courtroom testimony and concern would be shifted somewhat,

83

to bring to light environmental impacts that otherwise would go unnoticed; second, the appellate courts, through their review and reversals for "insufficient findings," would give content to, and build up a body of environmental rights, much as content and body has been given, over the years, to terms like "due process of law."

Beyond these procedural safeguards, would there be any rights of the environment deemed "absolute," at least to the extent that, say, free speech is absolute? Here, the doctrine of irreparable injury comes to mind. There has long been considerable support for an attorney general to enjoin injury to communal property (beaches, lakes) if he can prove the damage to be "irreparable." In other words, even in jurisdictions where repairable damage to the environment can be balanced and traded off against competing interests, there is a certain amount of legal doctrine suggesting that irreparable damage can be enjoined absolutely. There are several reasons why this doctrine has not been invoked effectively (witness Lake Erie). Undoubtedly, political pressures (in the broadest sense) have had an influence. So, too, has the failure of all of us to understand just how delicate the environmental balance is; this failure has made us unaware of (or unable to prove) just how early in the process of our ecological tampering "irreparable" injury was occuring. But most important, I think, is that the doctrine simply is not practical as a rule of universal application—and nothing is clearer in the history of the law than that when law and "necessity" collide, it is the law that gets bent (or riddled with the shrapnel of exceptions). There are too many cases like the sea urchin example, above, where the marginal costs of abating the damage to the environment seem too clearly to exceed the marginal benefits, even if the damage to the environment itself is liberally estimated. For another, there is a large problem in how one defines "irreversibly." Certainly the great bulk of the environment in civilized parts of the world has been injured "irreparably" in the sense of "irreversibly"; we are not likely to return it to its prehistoric quality. Thus, if we are going to revitalize the "irreparable damages" doctrine, and expect it to be applied consistently, distinctions are going to have to be made among environmental objects based upon judgments of their value to "us"—of an extended "us," however, one that includes the entire spaceship earth. What will be said to constitute "irreparable damage" to the ionosphere, because of its importance to all life, or to the Grand Canyon, because of its uniqueness, is going to rest upon practical and normative judgments that ought to be made explicit and subjected to public discussion.

This suggests that just as some of our justices feel there are "preferred constitutional rights" where humans are concerned, we establish an authoritative list of "preferred objects." Any threatened injury to these most-jealously-to-be-protected objects should be reviewed with the greatest degree of suspicion at all levels of government. Their "constitutional rights" should be implemented, legislatively and administratively, by the setting of environmental quality standards and similar measures.

Once the principal is admitted that natural objects have rights, other senses in which they might hold rights will become apparent and develop. (And, as I explain more fully below, these senses would be more apt to develop if only we should begin to *speak* in terms of their having rights, albeit vaguely at first.)

"Rights" might well lie in unanticipated areas. It would seem, for example, that Chief Justice Warren was only stating the obvious when he observed in *Reynolds v. Sims* (the great legislative reapportionment case) that "legislators represent people, not trees or acres." Yet, could not a case be made for a system of apportionment which *did* take into account the wildlife of an area? It strikes me as suspect that Alaska should have no more congressmen than Rhode Island primarily *because there are in Alaska all those trees and acres, those waterfalls and forests.* I am not saying that we ought to overrule *Baker v. Carr* and retreat from one man-one vote to a system of one man-or-tree, one vote. Nor am I even taking the position that we ought to count each acre, as we once counted each slave, as three-fifths of a man. But I am suggesting that there is nothing unthinkable about, and there might on balance even be a prevailing case to be made for, an electoral apportionment that made some systematic effort to allow for the representative "rights" of nonhuman life. And if a case might be made for a proposal as "far out" as that, I suspect that a society which grew concerned enough about the environment to make it a holder of rights would gradually work out quite a number of rights to have waiting for it when it got to court.

DO WE REALLY HAVE TO PUT IT THAT WAY?

At this point, one might well ask whether much of this could not be expressed without introducing the notion of trees, rivers, and so forth as "having rights." Couldn't we simply and straightforwardly lay down a body of legal rules which stated, for example, (R_1), that "the class of persons competent to challenge the pollution of rivers ought to be extended beyond that of persons who can show an immediate adverse economic impact on themselves;" and (R_2), that "judges, in weighing competing claims to a wilderness area, ought to think beyond the economic and even esthetic impact on man, and put into the balance a concern for the threatened environment as such." And it is true, indeed, that to say trees and rivers have "rights" is

87

not in itself a stroke of any operational significance—no more than to say "people have rights." As I have already noted, statements about rights are for a large part meta-legal—they are *descriptions* of a legal system (viewed from without), rather than elements of the system itself. To solve any concrete case, the law gradually has to spell out and apply increasingly precise and particularized statements, from which the word "right" itself might as well be, and usually is, dropped.

But to say this is not to suggest that introducing the notion of the "rights" of trees and rivers would accomplish nothing beyond the introduction of a set of particular rules like (R_1) and (R_2), above. Introducing the notion of something having a "right" (simply *speaking* that way), brings into the legal system a flexibility and open-endedness that no series of specifically stated legal rules of that sort can, or ought, fully to eliminate. Part of the reason is that "right" (and other so-called "legal terms" like "infant," "corporation," "reasonable time") carry meaning—vague, but forceful—in the ordinary language outside the courthouse walls, and the force of these meanings, crossing the boundary between ordinary and legal thought, becomes part of the context against which the legal language is interpteted.

Consider, for example, the rules that govern the question, on whom, and at what stages of litigation, is the burden of proof going to lie? Professor James Krier of U.C.L.A. has demonstrated how terribly significant these decisions are in the trial of environmental cases, and yet, also, how much discretion judges have under them. In the case of such vague rules (and all rules are more or less vague), it is *context*—senses of direction, of value and purpose—that determines how the rules will be understood, every bit as much as their supposed "plain meaning." In a society that spoke of the environment "having legal rights," judges would, I suspect, be inclined to interpret rules such as those of burden of proof far more liberally in favor of the environment. For the fact is, the vocabulary and expressions available to us always influence and even steer our thought. Consider the effect that was had by introducing into the law terms like "motive," "intent," and "due process." These terms worked a subtle shift into the rhetoric of explanation available to judges; with them, new ways of thinking and new insights have come to be explored and developed. In such fashion, judges who could unabashedly refer to the "legal rights of the environment" would be inclined to develop a viable body of law, in part simply through the availability and force of the expression.

Then, too, it is tempting to suppose that if only the law were to begin speaking of the environment's having legal rights, the notion would soon spill over beyond the courthouses into the popular consciousness (a prospect I am about to develop more fully); and a society so encouraged to think of the "legal rights of the environment" would presumably support more environment-protecting rules enacted through their legislatures.

If my interpretation of these influences is correct, then a society in which it is stated, however vaguely, that "rivers have legal rights" would evolve a different legal system than one which did not employ that expression, even if the two of them had, at the start, the very same "legal rules" in other respects.

⁊⊷ FOUR

Environmental Rights
and Social Consciousness

There are, as we have seen, a number of developments in the law that may reflect a shift
from the view that nature exists *for man*. These
range from increasingly favorable procedural rul-
ings for environmental action groups—regarding
standing and burden of proof requirements, for
example—to the enactment of comprehensive
legislation such as the National Environmental
Policy Act and the Michigan Environmental
Protection Act of 1970. Of such developments
one may say, however, that it is not the environment *per se* that we are prepared to take into
account, but that man's increased awareness of
possible long-range effects on himself militate in
the direction of arresting environmental harm in
its incipiency. Even the far-reaching National
Environmental Policy Act, in its preambulatory
"Declaration of National Environmental Policy,"

is ambivalent; it comes out both for "restoring and maintaining environmental quality *to the overall welfare and development of man*" as well as for creating and maintaining "conditions under which *man and nature can exist in productive harmony.*"

Because the health and well-being of mankind depend upon the health of the environment, these goals will often be so mutually supportive that one can avoid deciding whether our rationale is to advance "us" or a new extended "us" that includes the environment. For example, consider the Federal Insecticide, Fungicide, and Rodenticide Act (FIFRA) which insists that pesticides and other poisons include a warning "adequate to prevent injury to living man and other vertebrate animals, vegetation, and useful invertebrate animals." Such a provision undoubtedly reflects the sensible notion that the protection of humans is best accomplished by heading off dangerous accumulations early in the food chain. Its enactment does not necessarily augur far-reaching changes in, nor even call into question, fundamental matters of consciousness.

But the time is already upon us when we may have to consider subordinating some human claims to those of the environment *per se.* Consider, for example, the disputes over protecting wilderness areas from development that would make them accessible to greater numbers of people. I myself feel disingenuous defending the environmentalist's position in terms of a utilitarian calculus—the greatest good of the greatest number of people—even where the calculations take further generations into account, and play fast and loose with their definition of "good." Those who favor development have the stronger argument—they at least hold the protectionists to a standstill—so long as our touchstone be advancing the greatest good of the greatest number of people. And the same is true regarding arguments to preserve useless species of animals, as in my sea urchin hypothesis. One *can* say that we never know what is going to prove useful at some future time; and that we therefore ought to be conservative now in our treatment of nature, just to protect ourselves. I agree.

But when conservationists argue this way to the exclusion of other arguments, or find themselves speaking in terms of "recreational interests" so continuously as to play up to, and reinforce, anthropocentric perspectives, there is something sad about the spectacle. I expect the environmentalists want to say something less egoistic and more empathic but the prevailing and sanctioned modes of explanation in our society—our rhetorics of motive—are not quite ready for it. In just the same way, there must have been abolitionists who put their case for freeing the blacks on the grounds that *we* would thereby get more work out of them. Holdsworth says of the early English Jew that while he was "regarded as a species of *res nullius* . . . [h]e was

93

valuable for his acquisitive capacity; and for that reason the crown took him under its protection." Even today, businessmen are put in the position of apologizing that their decent but probably profitless acts are really designed to "help our company's reputation and be good for profits." (And, by the way, it is in no small measure the law, with its strictures on managerial largesse, that imposes on businessmen this twisted vocabulary of motive).

For my part, I would prefer a frank avowal that even allowing for derivative human benefits, what I am proposing is going to wind up costing "us," i.e., reducing our standard of living as measured in terms of our present values. And this frankness breeds a frank response—one which I hear from my colleagues and which must occur to many a reader. Insofar as the proposal goes beyond serving as an elaborate but practical legal fiction, and really comes down to compromising some of *our* interests for some of *theirs*, why should we adopt it? What's in it for "us"?

This is a matter I am prepared to address, but only after permitting myself some observations about how *odd* the question is—and how odd the form of my response needs be. The issue put this way, one is demanding a justification in the very anthropocentric hedonist terms that I am calling to question. One is inclined to respond, "Couldn't you (as a white) raise the same questions about compromising your preferred
94

rights-status with blacks?"; or "Couldn't you (as a man) raise the same question about compromising your preferred rights-status with women?" The problem is, if a move of this sort is right, it seems as though it should be right whether or not there's anything "in it" for anybody.

The dilemma is rooted in some fundamental characteristics of ethical argument. It is very hard to *prove* to someone that any other person or group deserves his consideration for its own sake. Arguments that attempt to do so on "neutral principles" almost inevitably engender covert appeals to the listener's self-interest. Recall that Socrates, who set himself up as an opponent of hedonistic thought, confuted Thrasymachus by arguing that immorality makes one miserably unhappy! Kant, who based his moral philosophy upon the categorical imperative ("Woe to him who creeps through the serpent windings of Utilitarianism") finds himself justifying, e.g., promise keeping and truth telling, on the most prudential—one might almost say, commercial —grounds. In the last analysis, such moral judgments may just have to (in Wittgenstein's phrase) "make themselves manifest."

With this reservation—that the task which follows is laden with what my colleague Morris Engel dubs "philosophic irony"—let me stress that the strongest case can be made from the perspective of human advantage for conferring rights on the environment. Scientists have been warning of the crises the earth and all humans on it face if we do not change our ways—radically—and these crises make the lost recreational use of rivers seem absolutely trivial. The earth's very atmosphere is threatened with frightening possibilities: absorption of sunlight, upon which the entire life cycle depends, may be diminished; the oceans may warm, increasing the "greenhouse effect" of the atmosphere, melting the polar ice caps, and destroying our great coastal cities. The portion of the atmosphere that shields us from cancer-inducing radiation is already on its way to destruction. Testifying before Congress, sea explorer Jacques Cousteau predicted that the oceans (to which we dreamily look to feed our booming populations) are headed toward their own death: "The cycle of life is intricately tied up with the cycle of water ... the water system has to remain alive if we are to remain alive on earth." We are depleting our energy and our food sources at a rate that takes little account of the needs even of humans now living.

These problems will not be solved easily; they very likely can be solved, if at all, only through a willingness to suspend the rate of increase in the standard of living (by present values) of the earth's "advanced" nations and by stabilizing the total human population. For some of us, this will involve forfeiting material comforts; for others, it will involve abandoning the hope someday to obtain comforts long envied. For all of us, it will involve giving up the right to have as many offspring as we might wish. Such a program is not impossible of realization, however. Many of our so-called "material comforts" are not only in excess of, but are probably in opposition to, basic biological needs. Further, the "costs" to the advanced nations is not as large as would appear from Gross National Product figures. G.N.P. reflects social gain (of a sort) without discounting the social cost of that gain, e.g., the losses through depletion of resources, pollution, and so forth. As has well been shown, as societies become more and more "advanced," their real marginal gains become less and less for each additional dollar of G.N.P. Thus, to give up "human progress" would not be as "costly" (even in terms of the values we presently measure) as might appear at first blush. It may even be a necessity.

But if we are going to undertake such far-reaching social changes, we are going to have to seriously reexamine our consciousness towards the environment. I say this knowing full well that there is something more than a trifle obscure in the claim. Is popular consciousness a meaningful notion, to begin with? If so, can anyone say what our present consciousness regarding the environment really is? Has it been causally responsible for our material state of affairs? Ought we to shift our consciousness (and if so, to what exactly, and on what grounds)? How, if at all, would a shift in consciousness be translated into tangible institutional reform? Not one of these questions can be answered to everyone's satisfactions, certainly not to the author's.

It is commonly being said today, for example, that our present state of affairs—at least in the West—can be traced to the view that Nature is the dominion of Man, and that this attitude, in turn, derives from our religious traditions. "Whatever the origins," Ian McHarg has written,

> the text is quite clear in Judaism, was absorbed all but unchanged into Christianity, and was inflated in Humanism to become the implicit attitude of Western man to Nature and the environment. Man is exclusively divine, all other creatures and things occupy lower and generally inconsequential stature; man is given dominion over all creatures and things; he is enjoined to subdue the earth . . . This environment was created by the man who believes that the cosmos is a pyramid erected to support man on its pinnacle, that reality exists only because man can perceive it, that God is made in the image of man, and that the world consists solely of a dialogue between men. Surely this is an infantilism which is unendurable. It is a residue from a past of inconsequence when a few puny men cried of their supremacy to an unhearing and uncaring world. One longs for a psychiatrist

who can assure man that his deep-seated cultural inferiority is no longer necessary or appropriate ... It is not really necessary to destroy nature in order to gain God's favor or even his undivided attention.*

Surely this is forcibly put, but it is not convincing as a full explanation for how we got to where we are. For one thing, so far as our present state of affairs are to be traced to intellectual (rather than material) influences, one might as fairly turn on Darwin as the Bible. It was, after all, Darwin's views—in part though the prism of Herbert Spencer—that gave moral approbation to struggle, conquest, and domination; indeed, by emphasizing man's development as a product of chance happenings and triumphs, Darwin also had the effect—intended or not—of reducing our awareness of the mutual interdependency of everything in Nature. And besides, as Earl F. Murphy points out, the spiritual beliefs of the Chinese and Indians "in the unity between man and nature had no greater effect than the contrary beliefs in Europe in producing a balance between man and his environment"; he claims that in China, *tao* notwithstanding, "ruthless deforestation has been continuous." I am under the impression too, that notwithstanding the vaunted "harmony" be-

*Ian McHarg, "Values, Process and Form," in *The Fitness of Man's Environment* (New York; Harper Colophon, 1970), pp. 213–14.

tween the American Plains Indians and Nature, once we had equipped them with rifles their pursuit of the buffalo gladly expanded to fill the potential of their awesome new technology.

The fact is, that "consciousness" explanations pass too quickly over simpler explanations: there is an increasing number of humans, with increasing wants, and there has been an increasing technology to satisfy them at some "cost" to the rest of nature. Thus, we ought not to place too much hope that a changed environmental consciousness will in and of itself reverse present trends. Furthermore, societies have long since passed the point where a change in human consciousness on any matter will rescue us from our problems. More than ever before, we are in the hands of institutions. These institutions cannot be brushed aside as "mere legal fictions," moreover—they have wills, minds, purposes, and inertias that are in very important ways *their own,* i.e., that can transcend and survive changes in the consciousnesses of the individual humans who supposedly comprise them, and whom they supposedly serve. (It is more and more the individual human being, with his consciousness, that is the legal fiction.)

For these reasons, it is far too pat to suppose that a western "environmental consciousness" is solely or even primarily responsible for our environmental crisis. On the other hand, it is not so extravagant to claim that it has dulled our resentment and our determination to respond. For this reason, our ability to bring about the requisite changes (in institutional arrangements, population growth, etc.) depends in part upon our developing and accepting new feelings about "our" place in the rest of nature.

A radical new conception of man's relationship to the rest of nature would not only be a step towards solving the material planetary problems. There are strong reasons for such a changed consciousness from the point of making us far better humans. If we only stop for a moment and look at the underlying human qualities that our present attitudes toward property and nature draw upon and reinforce, we have to be struck by how stultifying of our own personal growth and satisfaction they can become when they take rein of us. Hegel, in "justifying" private property, unwittingly reflects the tone and quality of some of the needs that are played upon:

> A person has as his substantive end the right of putting his will into any and every thing and thereby making it his, because it has no such end in itself and derives its destiny and soul from his will. This is the absolute right of appropriation which man has over all "things."

What is it within us that gives us this need not just to satisfy basic biological wants, but to extend our wills over things, to object-ify them,

101

to make them ours, to manipulate them? Can it all be explained on "rational" bases? Should we not be suspect of such needs within us, cautious as to why we wish to gratify them? When I first read that passage of Hegel, I immediately thought not only of the emotional contrast with Spinoza, but of the passage in Carson McCullers's Story, *A Tree, a Rock, a Cloud*, in which an old derelict has collared a twelve-year-old boy in a streetcar cafe. The old man asks whether the boy knows "how love should be begun?"

The old man leaned closer and whispered:
"A tree. A rock. A cloud. . . .

"At the time my science was begun. I meditated and I started very cautious. I would pick up something from the street and take it home with me. I bought a goldfish and I concentrated on the goldfish and I loved it. I graduated from one thing to another. Day by day I was getting this technique . . .

"For six years now I have gone around by myself and built up my science. And now I am a master. Son. I can love anything. No longer do I have to think about it even. I see a street full of people and a beautiful light comes in me. I watch a bird in the sky. Or I meet a traveler on the road.

Everything, Son. And anybody. All stranger and all loved! Do you realize what a science like mine can mean?"

To be able to get away from the view that Nature is a collection of useful but senseless objects is, as McCullers's "madman" suggests, deeply involved in the development of our abilities to love—or, if that is putting it too strongly, to be able to reach a heightened awareness of our own, and others' capacities in their mutual interplay. To do so, we have to give up some psychic investment in our sense of separateness and specialness in the universe. And this, in turn, is hard giving indeed, because it involves us in a flight backwards, into earlier stages of civilization and childhood in which we had to trust (and perhaps fear) our environment, for we had not then the power to master it. Yet, in doing so, we—as persons—gradually free ourselves of needs for supportive illusions. Is not this one of the triumphs for "us" of our giving legal rights to (or acknowledging the legal rights of) blacks and women?

Changes in this sort of consciousness are already developing, for the betterment of the planet and us. There is now federal legislation which "establishes by law" (one looks forward to the time when such behavior need not be "established by law" because it has become deeply enough rooted in decency and custom) the humane ethic that animals should be accorded the basic creature comforts of adequate housing, ample food and water, reasonable handling, decent sanitation, sufficient ventilation, shelter from extremes of weather and temperatures, and adequate veterinary care including the appropriate use of pain-killing drugs . . .*

The Vietnam war has contributed to this movement, as it has to others. Five years ago a Los Angeles mother turned out a poster which read "War Is Not Healthy for Children and Other Living Things." It caught on tremendously—at first, I suspect, because it was so clever as a protest against the war. But as people repeat such phrases, they begin to think about them, and the possibilities of what they have stumbled upon become manifest. In its suit against the Secretary of Agriculture to cancel the registration of DDT, Environmental Defense Fund alleged "biological injury to man and other living things." A few years ago the pollution of streams was thought of only as a problem of smelly, unsightly, unpotable water, i.e., a detriment to us. Now we are beginning to discover that pollution is a process that destroys wondrously subtle balances of life within the water, and as between the water and its banks. This heightened awareness enlarges our sense of

* Animal Welfare Act of 1970, 84 Stat. 1560, 7 U.S.C. § 2131 et. seq.

the dangers to us. But it also enlarges our empathy. We are not only developing the scientific capacity, but we are cultivating the personal capacities *within us* to recognize more and more the ways in which Nature—like the Woman, the Black, the Indian and the Alien—is like us. (And we will also become more able realistically to define, confront, live with and admire the ways in which we are all different).

The time may be on hand when these sentiments, and the early stirrings of the law, can be coalesced into a radical new theory or myth— felt as well as intellectualized—of man's relationships to the rest of nature. I do not mean "myth" in a demeaning sense of the term, but in the sense in which, at different times in history, our social "facts" and relationships have always been comprehended and integrated by reference to various "myths"—that we are cosigners of a social contract, that the pope is God's agent, that all men are created equal. Pantheism, Shinto and Tao all have myths to offer. But they are all, each in its own fashion, quaint, primitive and archaic to modern ears. What is needed is a myth that can fit our growing body of knowledge of geophysics, biology and the cosmos.

In this vein, I do not think it too remote that we may come to regard the Earth, as some have suggested, as one organism, of which Mankind is a functional part—the mind, perhaps: different from the rest of nature, but different as a man's brain is from his lungs. Dane Rudhyar, an astrol-

105

oger, composer, philosopher, and historian has written:

> Ever since the first Geophysical Year, international scientific studies have shown irrefutably that the Earth as a whole is an organized system of most closely interrelated and indeed interdependent activities. It is, in the broadest sense of the term, an "organism." The so-called life-kingdoms and the many vegetable and animal species are dependent upon each other for survival in a balanced condition of planet-wide existence; and they depend on their environment, conditioned by oceanic and atmospheric currents, and even more by the protective action of the ionosphere and many other factors which have definite rhythms of operation. Mankind is part of this organic planetary whole; and there can be no truly new global society, and perhaps in the present state of affairs no society at all, as long as man will not recognize, accept and enjoy the fact that mankind has a definite function to perform within this planetary organism of which it is an active part.
>
> In order to give a constructive meaning to the activities of human societies all over the globe, these activities—physical and mental—should be understood and given basic value with reference to the wholesome functioning of the entire Earth, and

we may add of the entire solar system. This cannot be done (1) if man insists on considering himself an alien Soul compelled to incarnate on this sorrowful planet, and (2) if we can see in the planet, Earth, nothing but a mass of material substances moved by mechanical laws, and in "life" nothing but a chance combination of molecular aggregations.

... As I see it, the Earth is only one organized "field" of activities—and so is the *human person*—but these activities take place at various levels, in different "spheres" of being and realms of consciousness. The lithosphere is not the biosphere, and the latter not the ... ionosphere. The Earth is not *only* a material mass. Consciousness is not only "human"; it exists at animal and vegetable levels, and most likely must be latent, or operating in some form, in the molecule and the atom; and all these diverse and in a sense hierarchical modes of activity and consciousness should be seen integrated in and perhaps transcended by an all-encompassing and "eonic" planetary Consciousness.

Mankind's function within the Earth-organism is to extract from the activities of all other operative systems within this organism the type of consciousness which we call "reflective" or "self-consciousness—or, we may also say to *mentalize* and give meaning, value, and "name" to all that takes place anywhere within the Earth-field ...

This "mentalization" process operates through what we call culture. To each region of, and living condition in the total field of the Earth-organism a definite type of culture inherently corresponds. Each region is the "womb" out of which a specific type of human mentality and culture can and sooner or later will emerge. All these cultures—past, present and future—and their complex interrelationships and interactions are the collective builders of the Mind of humanity; and this means of the *conscious Mind of the Earth.**

As radical as such a consciousness may sound today, all the dominant changes we see about us point in its direction. Consider just the impact of space travel, of worldwide mass media, of increasing scientific discoveries about the interrelatedness of all life processes. Is it any wonder that the term "spaceship earth" has so captured the popular imagination? The problems we have to confront are increasingly the worldwide crises of a global organism: not pollution of a stream, but pollution of the atmosphere and of the ocean. Increasingly, the death that occupies each human's imagination is not his own, but that of the entire life cycle of the planet Earth, to which each of us is as but a cell to a body.

To shift from such a lofty fancy as the planetarization of consciousness to the operation of our municipal legal system is to come down to earth hard. Before the forces that are at work, our highest court is but a frail and feeble—a distinctly human—institution. Yet, the Court may be at its best not in its work of handing down decrees, but at the very task that is called for: of summoning up from the human spirit the kindest and most generous and worthy ideas that abound there, giving them shape and reality and legitimacy. Witness the school desegregation cases which, more importantly than to integrate the schools (assuming they did so), awakened us to moral claims which, when made visible, could not be denied. And so here, too, in the case of the environment, the Supreme Court may find itself in a position to award "rights" in a way that will contribute to a change in popular consciousness. It would be a modest move, to be sure, but one in furtherance of a large goal: the future of the planet as we know it.

How far we are from such a state of affairs, where the law treats "environmental objects" as holders of legal rights, I cannot say. Certainly there were stirrings in this direction as early as 1970, in one of Justice Black's last dissents. Complaining of the Court's refusal to stay the Texas Highway Department's plan to run a six-lane expressway through a San Antonio park, Black observed that "after today's decision, the people of San Antonio and the birds and animals that make their home in the park will share their quiet retreat with an ugly, smelly stream of traffic ... Trees, shrubs, and flowers will be mown down." Elsewhere he wrote of the "burial of public parks," of segments of a highway which "devour parkland," and of the park's "heartland." Was he, at the end of his great career, on the verge of saying that "nature has 'rights' on its own account?"

The Mineral King opinions demonstrate that it would not be so hard to do. Perhaps as many as three Supreme Court justices have now indicated some willingness to accept legal claims presented in the name of a natural object. And while the balance of the Court has not yet been forced to reach the issue, it is only a matter of time before they must. Across the country, a small group of lawyers is already beginning to pick up the idea. A suit challenging inhumane methods of livestock slaughtering was brought in the name of "Helen E. Jones, as next friend and guardian for all livestock animals now and hereafter awaiting slaughter in the United States. . . ." Recently when the government planned to realign a road through a town common, a Massachusetts lawyer drafted a complaint in the name of, among others, "plaintiff the Billerica Common . . . a small park in the center of the town of Billerica." In the face of the threat (publicity-wise as well as legal) the government decided to withdraw the proposal. In 1974 a suit brought in the United States District Court for the District of Connecticut named the Byram River (which forms a portion of the boundary line between Connecticut and New York) one of the plaintiffs, demanding that at least thirteen years of intolerable pollution be abated. (*Byram River, et al. v. Village of Port Chester, New York, et al.*) United States District Judge John O. Newman denied defendants' motion to dismiss and transferred the case to the United States District Court for the Southern District of New York, where it is presently pending. In January 1975, a lawyer at a major New York firm named No Bottom Marsh and Brown Brook among two plaintiffs seeking relief in an antipollution suit filed in the same federal court. It, too, is presently awaiting disposition.

From my personal contact with the lawyers involved in these suits, as well as others who are drafting papers, I am certain that these cases are only the beginning. Perhaps the day is not too far off when the law will call us to account for—as Garrett Hardin puts it in his Introduction—our responsibilities as trustees of the earth.

Index

DISCUS BOOKS
DISTINGUISHED NON-FICTION

American Civil Liberties Union Handbooks on The Rights of Americans

THE RIGHTS OF MENTAL PATIENTS
Bruce Ennis and Loren Siegel
10652   1.25

THE RIGHTS OF THE POOR
Sylvia Law
18754   .95

THE RIGHTS OF PRISONERS
David Rusovsky
07591   .95

THE RIGHTS OF SERVICEMEN
Robert S. Rivkin
07500   .95

THE RIGHTS OF STUDENTS
Alan H. Levine and Eve Cary
05776   .95

THE RIGHTS OF SUSPECTS
Oliver Rosengart
18606   .95

THE RIGHTS OF TEACHERS
David Rubin
07518   .95

THE RIGHTS OF WOMEN
Susan Deller Ross
17285   1.25

THE RIGHTS OF REPORTERS
Joel M. Gora
21485   1.25

THE RIGHTS OF HOSPITAL PATIENTS
George J. Annas
22459   1.50

THE RIGHTS OF GAY PEOPLE   E. Carrington
Boggan, Marilyn G. Haft, Charles Lister, John P. Rupp   24976   1.75

Wherever better paperbacks are sold, or direct from the publisher. Include 25¢ per copy for mailing; allow three weeks for delivery.

Avon Books, Mail Order Dept.
250 West 55th Street, New York, N. Y. 10019

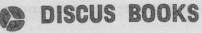

DISCUS BOOKS

DISTINGUISHED NON-FICTION

A SELECTION OF RECENT TITLES

DRT 7-75